The Last Four

God's Heart Unveiled: Prophetic Insight,
Warnings and Call to the Remnant

Kevin Winkler

This book was NOT written by AI, but by a real person with a real relationship with God.

The Last Four: God's Heart Unveiled: Prophetic Insight, Warnings and Call to the Remnant

ISBN: 979-8-9926539-5-3

Library of Congress Control Number: 2025923140

Cover design: Rachel Howarton (www.thechurchalive.com)

Published By: Winkler Writing Enterprise

www.winklerwritingenterpise.com

Printed in the United States of America

Contents

Acknowledgments

This is the second book I've had the privilege of writing and completing, and I say *privilege* on purpose.

Jesus, you are the One who deserves all praise and glory. You are the One who calls us to accomplish everything on earth of lasting value. Thank you, Lord, for your very real and gracious help. You are my best friend, and I am grateful to continue to grow in my relationship with You.

Lord, I do believe your way is to include others in our work, as others have a valuable part to play in our lives, our calling, and our accomplishments. I do believe you want us to acknowledge those people, too.

To my wife Misty, thank you for your continued and sustained support. You wrote this book too, as we are one. Thank you for your encouragement, my awesome wife! To my beloved daughter you are a very bright and beautiful person. I love you and I am so proud of the person in Christ you are becoming. I look forward to writing with you and also helping you publish your books.

Thank you to the entire Church Alive family! You continue to be a source of joy to me. Getting to be in a family relationship with you is an honor. Thank you for standing with us in support as we build this ministry together which gives me the opportunity to write!

Introduction

Do you believe God still speaks?

Do you believe that God cares about the challenges His children wrestle with in our modern culture?

If you do, then buckle up and prepare yourself to be encouraged and challenged!

This book is a collection of prophetic words that reflect the heart of a God who is faithful and involved. It's also a collection of lessons on Who is ultimately in charge. He rules from heaven, and no one–and I mean no one–can gain the upper hand against Him, no matter how hard they try. He is God, and that's just the way it is.

Each chapter in this book corresponds to a particular prophetic word given over a four-plus-year period. Together, they mark the official words I believe the Lord intended for me to speak to the global church. Of course, He was saying a lot of things to many different people (not just me), yet this marked my time to declare His words to the church as a whole, and to the world, alongside His other servants.

God wants to be known. He wants me to know Him, and He wants you to know Him.

I do not mean simply knowing *about* Him or holding some religious idea of Him (and there are a lot of nonsensical ideas of Him). He wants us to actually hear His voice and to feel His presence. He wants to show Himself strong in our lives and, through us, to let people see Him.

Having already prefaced that this book contains prophetic words, it's crucial for you to know that they are given to someone who has indeed met the man, Jesus Christ, and who has heard His voice.

The mantle Jesus gave for the prophetic office came to me in 2018, at a Wednesday night service. Our church was hosting a missionary couple, Reverend John and Angela Howarton. They were conducting the teaching part of our service. Our Wednesday gatherings were designed to go deeper than Sundays, and they attracted those who wanted more, so the atmosphere was different.

During the closing of the service, as I invited people forward for prayer, I felt the Lord say, "A mantle has fallen."

I thought, *a mantle has fallen off me?* The next day the Lord clarified (because I was concerned). "*On* you," He said. "A mantle has fallen *on* you." From that day forward, things began to change. I received the mantle, although I could not have guessed the depth of what the Lord would have me doing during one of the most difficult times in modern American history, and honestly, throughout the world. I began hearing His voice more clearly, as He communicated messages for me to share about what the world was about to experience and what He thought about it.

Yet I know that I was not the only one God raised up during that period. There were, and are, many others He uses to communicate His thoughts and His will for our generation.

As you turn the pages of this book, here are some important things to keep in mind:

- This book is divided into unit parts based on the year each message was given.
- Each chapter title reflects the theme of the word received.
- The prophetic words themselves have not been edited for content. Only grammar, spelling, and punctuation have been adjusted. I was very

careful as I wrote not to add anything of my own opinion, and if I began to, I quickly erased it.

- Whenever I do make comments before, during, or after these words, I clearly note that they are my own to avoid confusion.

Most importantly, it's important to remember that our ultimate source of truth is always the Bible. Any word we believe the Lord has shared with us must align with His revealed nature and character as written in Scripture. God still speaks individually, nationally, and globally if we are open to Him. Jesus said in John 10:26–27, "But you do not believe, because you are not of My sheep, as I said to you. My sheep hear My voice, and I know them, and they follow Me" (NKJV).

I'd like to conclude this introduction by briefly noting the difference between the gifts of the Spirit and the offices Christ has given His church. This will also help us to better understand what follows.

First Corinthians 12:4-11 teaches us that the Holy Spirit gives different gifts to every believer. These gifts are wisdom, knowledge, faith, healing, miracles, prophecy, discernment, tongues, interpretation and others. They are given for the benefit and building up of the body of Christ. Likewise, Ephesians 4:11–15 explains that Christ gave some as apostles, some as prophets, some as evangelists, some as pastors, and some as teachers. These offices are administrative roles designed to equip the saints, provide order, and bring unity.

The difference between gifts and offices is simple but important: gifts are given to all, but offices carry more responsibility. An office, given by Christ, is an administrative position for oversight to provide order and equip the saints to properly use their gifts. God is a God of order, and the offices help His people walk in maturity.

Can you imagine everyone trying to operate in their gifts without direction, clarity, or training? I've actually seen this to be a reality. There are a lot of people who operate in an out-of-control way in their gifts and don't think they need help or direction. Every gift God gives has to come through our souls, and our souls must be trained for us to be truly effective!

With this in mind, know that the words you're about to read were given to me as one who functions in the office of a prophet. The office of the prophet is, in part, like being a news reporter from heaven. I get to deliver the real facts of what is going on and what God intends to do.

Everything written and shared in these pages is what I believe God said, what I believe He has done, and what He is still going to do. You'll notice that I've included verses in parenthesis throughout the prophetic words. These verses reference different passages of the Bible that coincide with the specific prophetic words and show that they are biblically rooted.

It's not about me; it's all about Him. We, His creation, are vessels. We're jars of clay. To Him alone belongs the glory and praise for the great things He has done, is doing, and will do. Amen!

Now that you have this foundation, let us begin an incredible journey through *The Last Four.*

Chapter 1

The Beginning

WHERE DO I begin a book like this?

This is certainly different from my last book and is set apart from the others I hope to write in the future. The angle, the words, and the timing are unique, not only for this moment in human history, but also for the seasons to come.

For relevance, it seems right to start by giving some glimpses of my early relationship with God. This lays the groundwork for the prophetic words ahead by explaining how I came to believe He speaks and has spoken throughout my life.

I could start at the beginning of my life when I was still so little, maybe four or five years old.

At that time, my family was living in an apartment complex in Chula Vista, California. I remember being terrified of being left alone in my bedroom because at nap time, I would hear demonic creatures sliding around my bed. They were partially human with lizard-like heads and bodies and with appendages like tails. They would crawl, lift themselves up on their two arms, and slide across the floor. Their bodies made short *shhhhhhhh* sounds and sounded like they were sliding across the carpet. The sound was most likely from pulling their bodies, stopping, reaching forward, and pulling again.

I was petrified. I would cry out, insisting to my parents that there was a snake in the room. They would check, find nothing, and reassure me that I could go back to sleep. Yet, after they left, the sounds would return until I fell asleep from exhaustion.

These encounters marked me deeply, long before I could even understand anything about the spiritual world and certainly long before the grown-ups in my life could fathom that a child could be bothered by unseen forces. When I was older, my mother told me that witchcraft had been practiced heavily in that complex. After we moved, the experiences stopped, but they had already left a mark on my life.

I could also begin this book by recounting the time I lined up stuffed animals on the stairwell of another apartment complex and preached to them (hey, the stuffies needed saving, too!). Or when I, as a kindergartner, stood on the church stage and loudly delivered my version of the Ten Commandments to an empty sanctuary. Our pastor, who was babysitting me and my brother at the time, paused a marriage counseling session to listen.

Maybe I should begin when I was in third grade. I had started to learn that Jesus was my best friend and that He hears our prayers. We did not have a lot of money, and I decided to ask Jesus for new bikes for me and my siblings since ours were getting worn out. In the mid-seventies, bikes were the main mode of transportation for kids.

At first, in childlike faith, I asked Jesus for a magic wand. "Jesus, can you make me a magic wand and put it on the ground right here in front of me so that I can make myself a new bike?' I asked. "I'm going to close my eyes and turn around. When I open my eyes, and turn back, you can have the wand on the ground."

I fully expected to see a magic wand on the ground. After all, He said to ask, and I was asking, right?

Well, I turned around and guess what I found? Absolutely nothing, nope, nada! No wand ever appeared. I thought He might need more time, or that I would have to repeat myself many times before it happened. I asked again and again... but still, no magic wand.

Three months later, on Christmas morning, our stepdad sternly told us (as he had many times before) to move our bikes out of the driveway. Puzzled, we said, "Dad, we didn't leave our bikes out there."

We were confused. "Dad, we did not leave our bike out there... We did not...."

"Bikes... Whaaaa..." It slowly was dawning on us as we looked out the front window at our driveway. There before our very eyes three brand new, cool, rad, glistening-in-the-morning-sunlight bikes, strategically placed in a way that would show off their glorious majesty!

We ran outside to check them out and wow! It was like getting a new car with all the features—mag wheels, handlebar pads, and knobby tires, and no multi-colored handlebar streamers and banana seat!

And then we realized we had not put any pants on in our haste to get outside... It was a little drafty.

So, needless to say, that first order of business before we could fully try them out was to get dressed!

Jesus had not given me a magic wand. He answered in a way only He could—through parents who didn't have the money, but somehow made it happen. The Lord made sure it would be answered through my parents because He responds to childlike faith.

That answered prayer left an indelible mark: God hears, God sees, and God provides.

When I was twelve years old, on a summer morning, I walked to my grandparents' pond to fish at their farm. I looked around at the beauty. The sunshine peeked through the trees, birdsong's filled the air, and the day just felt fresh. I said aloud, "Jesus, this day is so beautiful."

Then came His audible reply: "I am glad you like it."

There was nothing weird or startling about this encounter; it was just simple and real.

Over the years there were many similar encounters. Many more than I could recount to you in these limited pages.

Why do I take the time to recount my "prophetic credentials?" Simply to demonstrate that my relationship with Him has been cultivated over the course of my life. I am not someone who just recently started "hearing" from the Lord; I have learned what His voice sounds like over time.

Like the prophet Jeremiah's experience with the Lord, Jeremiah 1:4–10 reminds us that God appoints and sets people apart even before birth. I don't compare myself to Jeremiah, but I know this: the Lord has called me, not because of my perfection, but because of His mercy.

I want to be clear: my journey has not been perfect. I've made a mess of things, and like many people, I've wandered. There were "dangerous years" when I went astray, falling into sin and walking away from Him. During this time, I was shaken awake by Hebrews 10:26–27 which says,

"If we deliberately keep on sinning after we have received the knowledge of the truth, no sacrifice for sins is left, but only a fearful expectation of judgment and of raging fire that will consume the enemies of God."

This Scripture drew me back to the Lord because the reality of judgment terrified me. Even in the midst of running from God, He pursued me and tried to help me to keep following Him, and I responded by repenting of my sins, yielding to Him, and giving Him my obedience and trust.

Romans 3:23 reminds us: "For all have sinned and fall short of the glory of God." This is why none of us can ever condemn others for falling backwards. Even the angels–those who were in God's very presence–chose to rebel. Without God's active role in our lives, I believe we would find it hard to resist the devil. Romans 3:10-12 says,

"None is righteous, just and truthful and upright and conscientious, no, not one. No one understands [no one intelligently discerns or comprehends]; no one seeks out God. All have turned aside; together they have gone wrong and have become unprofitable and worthless; no one does right, not even one!" (AMPC)

God has mercy on us and will forgive us if we truly come to Him and repent. I repented, gave my life fully to Him, and finally surrendered to His question: *"Do you yield to Me?"* My answer was yes, and everything started to change. Two weeks later I was filled with the Spirit at an altar call at church, and my life began on an upward trajectory ever since that day.

Looking back, twenty-six years later at the writing of this book, I see how His hand was weaving through my entire life. Even when I resisted Him, He pursued me. He was faithful during those early years of training and hearing His voice, and He has continued to be faithful during the testing and training I've endured in the years since. But to have Him has been worth it, and those who have truly yielded to Him have this same testimony.

Why share these childhood memories, youthful encounters, and struggles? Because they reveal the steady presence of God, the shaping of His hand over time, and the foundation for the prophetic words that follow. I share them also to show that these words did not arrive in a vacuum. They came through a life God had been pursuing and preparing since childhood.

What you are about to read rests on this truth: God is faithful, He still speaks, and His purposes stretch across a lifetime. He will never leave us, no matter what our world looks like and what seems insurmountable. If we look to Him, we will find peace and hope in the midst of chaos and confusion.

He is Lord, forever and ever more.

Part One

2020 | *What's Coming!*

Section Notes

Little did we know what was coming when 2020 started.

At that time, we were at the early onset of COVID-19, a diabolical weapon used on the world by our enemies. That's my belief and opinion, formed after everything we've learned.

Many of us were locked down at home. We couldn't go to work, some of our churches were only hosting services online, and our social lives were very limited. Yet we had no idea that there was still more to come.

What most of us also didn't realize was that this moment in human history would mark a turning point—a marker on God's timeline of events.

Without divine help, how could anyone truly discern what the enemy was planning or what God was about to do? The world truly seemed to be turned upside down. Our human senses were not enough to guide us through the confusion. We needed something more; we needed knowledge and understanding from beyond human reasoning or the mainstream media!

Where does "more" come from? The answer lives in our Creator and Lord. From His being flows the "more" we so desperately need.

Proverbs 16:1 says, "The plans of the mind and orderly thinking belong to man, but from the Lord comes the [wise] answer of the tongue" (AMPC). God gave us minds capable of reasoning, planning, and creating, but our understanding is limited. We often act without all the facts, and we need His voice to fill in what our senses cannot.

Jesus affirmed this truth in Matthew 4:4, saying, "It has been written, Man shall not live and be upheld and sustained by bread alone, but by every word that comes forth from the mouth of God" (AMPC). In this verse, He was pointing out that life is sustained not only by physical means, but by spiritual nourishment, which is God's Word.

We need the Lord to help us understand what is happening behind the veil. We live in physical bodies, but we are spiritual beings. While God made us in His image and gave us some of His divine attributes, such as creativity, planning, and problem-solving, we are not God. We don't know everything, and we cannot sustain ourselves without Him.

Proverbs 3:5 reminds us of this, saying, "Lean on, trust in, and be confident in the Lord with all your heart and mind and do not rely on your own insight or understanding" (AMPC).

In short, there is worldly wisdom and there is divine wisdom. There are visible realities and unseen spiritual forces working, and it's crucial for every believer to understand this.

We must also recognize that God will bring this current age to an end. After that, there will remain only His kingdom and a place forever separated from Him (and none of us want to be in that place).

While we are here, living in our lives, both kingdoms are at work. There are plans and purposes made by the kingdom of darkness, carried out by its wicked ruler, Satan. But there are also divine plans from the kingdom of light, which is ruled by Jesus, the King of Kings.

God has not left us without help. He is ultimately in charge, and His purposes will prevail. In fact, Psalm 33:10 says, "The Lord brings the counsel of the nations to nought; He makes the thoughts and plans of the peoples of no effect" (AMPC). Likewise, Proverbs 19:21 confirms, "Many are the plans in a person's heart, but it is the Lord's purpose that prevails."

Thinking back on the years 2020 through 2024, I think we can all say, "What a season *that* was." We endured fear, uncertainty, misinformation, and deception on a scale the world had never seen. The questions many of us quietly asked were:

- Would America survive for another season?
- Would the world come to an end now?
- Would God allow us more time?
- Would we ever laugh again?
- Would we see hope–any silver lining–on this side of eternity?

If we had only looked at what was happening in the natural world, we might have concluded that the answer to all of these questions was *no*.

But what was *God* saying? What were *His* plans? Did He have anything to say at all?

He did, and He was speaking. In fact, He was issuing His Word more clearly than we had heard in years! Those holding the office of the prophet, the "news reporters" of heaven, were being awakened and released in masses.

They began sharing messages that, at the time, seemed impossible! And yet here we are, still standing, with restored hope and renewed understanding.

That's what this book represents: heaven's reports during one of the most turbulent times in modern history. I am honored to have been part of this master plan and still be part of it today.

To God be the glory.

Chapter 2

Distinction

March 31, 2020

THE LORD OFTEN ALLUDES TO "DISTINCTIONS" in Scripture. This refers to invisible lines that separate those who are His from those who aren't. We can see this in Exodus 8:23, for example, when He says to Pharaoh through Moses, "I will make a distinction between My people and your people." This was a tangible separation between the Egyptians and the Israelites, and it couldn't have been clearer. Plagues fell on Egypt, one after another, but skipped over the land of Goshen and the people of God. Judgment came to the wicked and passed over the righteous.

This theme runs throughout God's Word. Malachi 3:18 promises, "You will again see the distinction between the righteous and the wicked, between those who serve God and those who do not." Jesus emphasizes this in Matthew 25: 31-33, when He speaks of separating the sheep from the goats. God makes it clear: He knows those who belong to Him, and He has a way of making that known to the rest of the world.

In 2020, as the world was suddenly thrown into upheaval by the COVID-19 lockdowns and the uncertainty they brought, this distinction became something the body of Christ had to lean on. We faced worldwide turmoil and walked through frustration, yet what I didn't know was that God was about to declare that we'd already won.

Many were unable to see this because there were other competing voices speaking into what was happening. In fact, there are generally three voices going on inside of us at any given time (and sometimes all at once): God's, the enemy's, and our own. God wants us to be in tune with His voice, and this is one of the reasons He wants us to spend time with Him in His Word and prayer. He never contradicts His Word or His nature, so we must learn to distinguish His voice from others.

As I spent time trying to hear what God had to say about COVID-19, this is what I believe God spoke to my heart at the end of March 2020:

- *The Message* -

I believe that God indicated that "around" the beginning of May, we will see things start getting better—a return to some normality. It is most likely going to take most of the summer to stabilize the economy and bring everything back "RIGHT ON TIME" (there was an emphasis here). We will be okay, despite the news reports.

Don't give in to fear! Look how God is protecting the godly. Look how God is dealing with the wicked. If there is such a distinction now between the people, what do you think it will be like in the "real end?" (Exodus 8:23; Malachi 3:18; Matthew 25:31 [AMPC])

The real end has not come yet! But God is getting us ready for it.

The Lord saying "Do not give in to fear" references Isaiah 41:10, which states, "So do not fear, for I am with you; do not be dismayed, for I am your God. I will strengthen you and help you; I will uphold you with my righteous right hand." God's heart has always been to calm His people in the middle of storms, whether they were facing threats from enemies or, as in our case, a global pandemic. We can take comfort in the fact that God is not a distant observer. He is active and wants to speak to what is happening on earth, no matter what we see, for His glory and our good.

If we fast forward to today, we can see that God was absolutely right: we are here and what is happening in the world shows the proof that we had truly already won. This prophetic word, that God makes a distinction, is both an encouragement and a warning. It's imperative that we find ourselves on the right side–His side–right now. There is no time to lose.

Chapter 3

The Time Ahead

August 13, 2020

GOD HAS ALWAYS SPOKEN to His people about "the time ahead." In Genesis 6:13-18, Noah was warned about the flood long before it came. Likewise, Joseph interpreted Pharaoh's dream regarding seven years of plenty and seven years of famine and even provided a solution for surviving (Genesis 41:25-32). Lastly, Jesus Himself gave His disciples clear signs about what would happen in the last days (Matthew 24).

When the Lord gave me this word in August of 2020, I was gaining more confidence in writing what I believed I was hearing from the Lord. It was the second message I received from Him about this season of time.

I know that prophecy works on two levels; it speaks to the *now* and it speaks to the *not yet*. We see this in Isaiah 7:14, where God spoke to King Ahaz about His deliverance, but His words also pointed to the birth of Jesus.

Likewise, this prophetic word was both comfort for the immediate crisis of 2020 and a preview of what was still to come.

- *The Message* -

"Be of good cheer, I have overcome the world for you. Do not be startled at what the enemy is trying to do. He has lost! (John 16:33)

I love you, my church! I want the best for you always. It's never My will to hurt you, but to mature you in My likeness. Sometimes, My discipline can seem strong, but it is always given out of My love for you. Please accept it and learn My ways. My ways are ways of peace and joy, love and contentment. My ways are not hard, sharp, or uncaring." (Ephesians 5:25; Hosea 2:19-21; Matthew 11:28-30)

The Lord here echoes Jesus' words in John 16:33: "In this world you will have trouble. But take heart! I have overcome the world." God doesn't just want us to survive hardship. He wants us to live in the assurance that He is with us, in us, and that the outcome is already decided.

I think it's also interesting to note that He links discipline with love. Hebrews 12:6 says that the Lord "disciplines those He loves, and He chastens everyone He accepts as a son." This means that when God corrects us, it's not Him being cruel; it's an act of mercy to make us more like Christ.

"I will always provide for My bride, but My bride must listen to My instructions and heed them. If I lead in a way that does not seem right to you, My Spirit will give you that discernment to take a step anyway. I will never lead you to go against My Father's will or wishes.

I am bringing great discernment into the world. People who have never seen the true condition of their society are being shown. Those who did not want to know will know. There is a time of judgment coming that will make way for a great time of peace and prosperity that this world has never known previously. This time of great blessing is intended to make room for My harvest.

So do not despair when the world is also shaken by the exposure of corruption. Many men have given themselves over to wickedness and destruction, but My bride shall understand that I am Lord and there is no other. I rule from heaven; I give authority, I give direction, I give blessing, I call things that are not as though they are! (Romans 4:17)

I will instruct you, My church, individually on what you're to do as these things are brought to the light. To one I may ask to do this, to another I may ask to do that, but together it will create a strong body, with all functioning together. (1 Corinthians 12:1-30)

To My individual people: what does the Spirit say? What are you hearing in your inner man? What is being spoken in your heart as we approach the election of the U.S. President? Does My Spirit speak of panicking? Does My Spirit cause you to fear or be afraid? Does my Spirit nudge you with wisdom to be prepared for the exposure of evil? Does my Spirit move you to make arrangements practically to care for your bodily needs for a very short season? Does My Spirit move on you to make arrangements for the needs of others, too?

As I have spoken, I will always take care of My bride, but My bride must be listening and responding to Me.

I know all! I see all!

Take courage My church, I love you."

Notice the questions He asks here. He is asking His people to identify what His Spirit is saying in the midst of what's happening in the world. Again, there are always competing voices for any given situation, and we as God's people must know what His Spirit says about each situation. Likewise, the reminder I felt He gave about the upcoming election shows how specific He can be. Just like He appointed Cyrus in Isaiah 45 and Nebuchadnezzar in Jeremiah 27 to serve His purposes, He is still involved in raising leaders and shaping nations.

Finally, He closes with love. Everything He does flows from His love–His correction, His instructions, and even His warnings. When you see what has taken place in the world since this prophetic word was given, we could say that this was both for the 2020 and the 2024 election. As I have read and re-read this passage over the years, I am still amazed, though not surprised, at how specifically God speaks into situations before they take place.

Part Two

2021 | The Dark Valley

Section Notes

We will not spend very much time in this section as most of the following chapters are self-explanatory. Pay careful attention to the progression through the years, as God unfolds His plans.

Chapter 4

My Judgements are Final

January 1, 2021

THERE ARE times when God moves in mercy and provides time for people and nations to repent. Then there are times when His patience reaches its fullness and His judgments are revealed.

We see this in Genesis 6:3. God gave decades of warning before Noah and his family boarded the ark, and when He shut the doors, it wasn't long before all other human life ended. In contrast, when Jonah delivered the message of repentance to Ninevah, we see God withholding the judgment He had intended (Jonah 3:10).

God does not judge as man judges. While human judgment can be partial, political, and corrupt, He judges in fairness and according to His love and mercy. As 2021 dawned, the Lord was speaking clearly about His judgments and the difference between those who walk with Him and those who resist Him.

We were just coming off of deep uncertainty in our nation. The wicked looked like they had won and that all was lost. We were neck-deep in COVID-19 and what looked like a questionable election when this prophetic word came, and the words were like water to a thirsty soul.

- *The Message* -

"My judgments are final. What I have declared I will bring to pass. My name will be praised in the heavens and the earth. Look up people, My children, and see the hand of the Most-High raised in victory (Proverbs 19:21; Psalms 118:16).

Does not the Lord reign? Does He not rule? (Psalms 47:8; Psalms 9:7)

My appointed shall crush his enemies. He shall not hold back the destruction I have decreed against the evil doers. (John 15:16; Ezekiel 3:17)

I love those who love righteousness. I keep those who desire truth in their inner beings. Why would I leave them to the devices of their enemies when they belong to Me? No, the day has finally come. (Psalms 91; 2 Kings 17:39)

I say to My true sons and daughters, 'Do not be afraid.'"

This word came at the beginning of a four-year fight of faith. How could we have truly known then that President Trump–God's appointed president–would ever be allowed by the wicked to enter the White House again?

For some, even the name "Trump" stirs up negative emotions. Why is this? What is the reason for feeling this way toward him? I did not pick him, and you did not pick him. God picked him, like he picked the judges of old. Is God not allowed to choose whomever He wills to do His work? Before his predecessor's term had even ended, God was declaring who He chose and who would crush His enemies in the future!

This word also reminds us that while human plans rise and fall, God's decrees stand firm forever. His judgments are not cruel, but instead, they combine mercy and truth. Looking back on the years since this word was given, it's clear that God was both warning and comforting His people. The same hand that judges evil will also shield those who love Him.

There's also a personal call here: we need to align ourselves with His righteousness and love truth so we can stay steady when the world trembles. As we move to the next message, let's keep in mind: when God talks about justice, He is also preparing mercy.

Chapter 5

I Want My Church to be a Part of This

February 20, 2021

THERE ARE moments in history when God makes clear that though the battle is already settled in heaven, He wants His people to rise and participate on earth. Scripture is full of these types of moments, For instance, when Israel stood before the town of Jericho in Joshua 6:2, God declared, "See, I have delivered Jericho into your hands." For their part, however, they still had to march.

In 2 Chronicles 20:15, we see another example of this in Jehoshaphat's life. When he faced overwhelming armies, the prophet declared, "The battle is not yours, but God's." Even so, the people still had to stand firm in faith.

Going forward, God gave a word almost every month at this time. I didn't plan for this, but boy, did I need it. When you look at what He shared, how could anyone know what He was doing behind the scenes and what His plans were? The victory had already been decided, but we still had a part to play.

- *The Message* -

"I want My church to be a part of this!

The battle has already been decided; it's already been won (Revelation 17:14). This is no longer about the enemy, that's been decided! This is about the church getting on board and staying on board with what God wants and is doing!

Does the church not have power anymore? Are the kings and priests of the earth powerless to affect change or proclaim what God has decreed?

God is allowing there to be a moment in time, given to the church, to get on His side" (Exodus 32:26).

This echoes Revelation 17:14, where the angel told John, "They will wage war against the Lamb, but the Lamb will triumph over them because He is the Lord of Lords and King of Kings and with Him will be His called, chosen and faithful followers." The victory is Christ's, but the church is called to stand with Him in that triumph.

The reference to the church getting "on His side" reminds us of Moses' call after Israel's rebellion with the golden calf. He said in Exodus 32:26, "Whoever is for the Lord, come to me." In His mind-boggling mercy, God gave His people a moment to choose sides. Likewise, this prophetic word declared that the church was being given another such moment to "make a decision" as to which side they want to be on.

Special note: I feel like this next paragraph could very well be a mixture of my own thoughts and feelings as I was sensing the message. I did my very best not to proclaim something as God's Word when it was my own. Allow the Holy Spirit to help you discern what is for you.

Where is God and with whom is He with? Act like it! This is not about criminals anymore. They have had time to come forward and repent. God gave them many ways out. God has had mercy, that time is now over (Genesis 15:16; Luke 13:1-9; Isaiah 55:6). They will be brought forward to account.

Again, I say this is about the weak and impotent church not standing up and at least praying, not praying for the enemy, but for God to bring about what He has declared. (According to Ecclesiastes there is a time and place for everything under the sun. There are Scriptures that say, "pray for your enemy and those who persecute you." Yes, we do pray for their ultimate salvation, but we're not praying for their success. We're praying that God removes them.)

It does not matter to Him whether you believe in the other offices of the church that He set forth and designed to train, edify, admonish, and encourage the body. Your leaders have failed you by not teaching you these things. Whether you're one denomination or another, the Word in its entirety is for all (2 Timothy 3:16-17). What have My true prophets said? What have they declared? What is the going thread within these words? What has God decreed and declared? It does not matter who says what! It does not matter who tries to stop it! God has said what He has said and He will do what He will do!

The references here are striking and make it clear that there is a time when mercy expires and accountability sets in. In Genesis 15:16, God told Abram that judgment would come on the Amorites when "the sin of the Amorites has reached its full measure." This shows us that although God is rich in mercy, there is an appointed limit before justice must come. Similarly, Luke 13:1-9 shows Jesus issuing a warning that unless people repent, they will perish.

For the church, the charge given in this prophetic word is to pray in alignment with God's decrees so that His righteous purposes may prevail. While the church may currently struggle with denominational divides, 2 Timothy 3:16-17 tells us that all Scripture is "God-breathed." God's Word, whether given through Scripture or through His prophets, cannot be undone.

I'm so glad God chooses to work through His church body. He doesn't have to operate this way. He created all things by His mighty power and holds it all together by His Word. It's mind-blowing to think that while He could do it all by Himself, He has called us into being and invited us to be a part of His plans.

God declared His plans for the enemy. He wants us to focus on our authority and power through Him as the body of Christ. He wants us to exercise our power to "do something" about the situation because He wants us to win! He will act even if we don't, but He wants us to learn to operate in our places as kings and priests of the earth.

Chapter 6

Hold On!

April 16, 2021

BY APRIL 2021, many believers were weary. The excitement of "God is moving" had by this time worn into the reality of waiting. The church was watching events unfold, most of the time with doubt, confusion, and fatigue. God knew we were growing weary and that it was still going to take several years for Him to put things in place.

Scriptures show us that God often speaks the most powerfully when His people are at their weakest. He acknowledges our weakness and calls us to endurance by pointing out that He wants to walk closely with us through hard things. First Kings 19:3-12 shows us when Elijah, after a great victory, collapsed under discouragement. God whispered to Him, revealing just how near He is. He does so in this word as well.

- *The Message* -

"I know you are wavering. I know your strength is weakening. I know this is long but hold on. What God has in store for the wicked is indeed terrifying. But righteousness will always prevail" (John 1:5).

. . .

Kevin Winkler

Here, God recognizes the condition of His people. He sees their works and endurance as well as their fatigue. No matter how long the "night" season seems, righteousness will prevail because Christ is the Light.

"Where is my hand working? Where are the signs of my doings? Can you see them? Are you awake and watching?

What am I doing, My church? Do you know? Are you paying any attention? Has your strength failed you? Has your resolve been dissolved?

I laugh at those who say, 'It is over.'"

"Hah!" says the Lord. "No, it's not over and you don't win!" (my note: He is talking to the enemy)

"My glorious name will be praised from the roof tops! My hand will be clearly seen by all. You think this is the end? No, it's not. I say when the end is, that is reserved for Me," says the Lord – "Not you, not them, not anyone. If I want to keep you 1000 years I can (John 21:22).

Who can see what I am doing from the beginning to the end? (Ecclesiastes 3:11; Isaiah 46:10)

Shall My Spirit be hindered by mere man? Shall My Word be thwarted? Who can stand against Me and live? I hold all life in My hands" (Acts 17:28).

God is sovereign over history. In John 21:22, Jesus said to Peter about John, "If I want him to remain alive until I return, what is that to you? You must follow me." In other words, God directs the steps of the righteous and sets the times and seasons, not man. Ecclesiastes confirms this, saying, "He has made everything beautiful in its time. He has also set eternity in the human heart; yet no one can fathom what God has done from beginning to end."

"You say, 'Where are You?' Look around and see Me everywhere.

I love you. Don't be dismayed. Don't be agitated by the wicked; they have no substance, they are hollow and empty, mere beasts—really! A pitiful sight.

Yet they can run to Me at any time. O' how great is My mercy and lovingkindness to those who repent, to those who walk away from evil and surrender. How loving are My ways to them! But woe to those who keep to their own path, who do harm to My church, to My bride; their days are truly numbered and none of them who stay their course will survive" (2 Peter 2:12; Psalms 145:8; Psalms 1:5).

"I the Lord have spoken! I the Lord am He that lives forever and ever in the eternity of eternities. Everlasting AM I.

Seek peace for yourself through the comforts of the Lord. Why be all wrought-up? (Psalms 34:14)

"Why be dismayed? Did I not say what I will do?

Seek comfort in Me and rest without becoming weary.

I love those who love Me. I carry those who seek truth. I am an advocate to those who stand with Me (Matthew 12:30).

Be patient. You are mine and I am yours. Ask whatever you want from Me and it will be yours.

Stay calm, stay focused.

Do your part by walking in faith, hope, love.

Let Me deal with them. I will help you amass an army of saints to walk in victory! (Revelations 19:14)

Can I help you? Please let Me. I want to (Psalms 37:5-17).

You pray, you stay in faith, you stay in hope, you stay in love (1 Corinthians 13:13).

Be a voice of cheer to the weary and a strength for the brokenhearted (Psalms 147:3).

Your love is precious to Me. Use it to strengthen others.

I the Lord have spoken!"

. . .

Psalm 37 reminds us to commit our ways to the Lord and to trust Him in confidence that He will act. This word closes with both a commission and an affirmation: strengthen the weary, cheer up the brokenhearted, and know that your love is precious to God. It's both a comfort and a correction; God sees our weariness and reminds us that His plan is unfolding on His timetable, not ours. He reassures us of His sovereignty while also calling us to endure in faith, hope, and love.

The heart of the message is that we are not to give up. Even after He speaks victory over a situation, the storm may still rage and the wicked may still boast, yet He will continue to provide encouragement and comfort as we trust in Him.

Chapter 7

A New Era: A New Day Has Begun

May 18, 2021

BY THIS TIME, many were still wondering when things would begin to change. Restrictions had recently been lifted regarding mask-wearing and the stay-at-home order, but when would we see a return to normality?

Well, the Lord was already declaring that a new day had begun.

This is something God has repeatedly done throughout history. He often proclaims a shift in the spirit realm before it manifests in the natural. For instance, Isaiah 43:19 declares, "See, I am doing a new thing! Now it springs up; do you not perceive it?" When God announces a new thing, it is already established in heaven, even if the earth hasn't yet caught up.

What did it mean that a new day had begun? What was God up to and how was He going to fix all of this mess in the world?

- *The Message* -

God is listening to the people, the people He loves (Malachi 3:16-18). Do you really believe that He was going to let this go on? These people are evil and wicked, utterly useless, and utterly destitute (2 Peter 3:4). He has spoken; He will reveal their plans. The world will be shocked yet again. (Luke 8:17)

Malachi 3:16-18 reminds us that God hears the conversations and prayers of those who fear Him and records them in His "book of remembrance." Here, the Lord affirms that He has been listening to "the people He loves," those who cried out for relief and an end to the pandemic. Luke 8:17 confirms His justice, declaring that "there is nothing hidden that will not be disclosed." God will not allow injustice and corruption to remain buried forever. He brings all the things to light.

How many times has the Lord, in knowledge, reached out to plead with them to repent, not wanting them to perish? They refuse to listen; they close their ears to His loving hand (Proverbs 21:13). God knows we are subject to the assaults of temptation, that our hearts are born sinful—but He made a divine way to be re-created and to be born again with hope (1 Corinthians 10:13). Woe to you workers of iniquity. Woe to you Sodom and Gomorrah. Woe to you Babylon. Woe to you who closed your eyes to evil when you knew what to do and did not do it!

God's mercy has always preceded His judgment. Peter wrote that God does "not [want] anyone to perish, but everyone to come to repentance" (2 Peter 3:9). God's nature is to be merciful. The Bible tells us that He is rich in mercy (Ephesians 2:4), but because people don't respond to His mercy, they often face judgment. Likewise, 1 Corinthians 10:13 reminds us that God provides a way out of temptation, but refusing His way also leads to judgment. The repeated "woe" statements echo Jesus's own words about the religious leaders in Matthew 23. God is clear; evil has a limit.

"Where is My hand now? I will do it without you. Do you think your inactivity will stop Me? I created all things without your involvement. I do as I please. For I, the Lord, am He who rules the heavens and the earth, the seas and skies and all that they contain (Matthew 28:18).

By My Word were the heavens created and by My Word will they be replaced (John 1:1-3). I will accomplish what I have set out to do. What are my signs of My working? Did you not receive the last ones? What have the prophets spoken, what have been the signs indicating My moving? What has come to pass? What is still pending My orders? Keep your eyes on what I have said. These are for you, so that you will believe. I have spoken, then I have performed what I have said, so that you would not doubt that there is a God in heaven, who knows all, sees all, and who is fully able to act! I, the Lord, have spoken."

This reflects Isaiah 55:11:

"So is my word that goes out from my mouth: It will not return to me empty but will accomplish what I desire and achieve the purpose for which I sent it."

As I have read and re-read this chapter, I have asked myself: *What was the Lord trying to communicate to us?* Considering everything that's happened since this was released, we can say that God truly calls things that are not as though they are!

God was pointing His people to the signs already fulfilled as evidence that He will continue to perform His Word. This word signals a turning point; God was announcing that a new era had already begun, even if it wasn't yet visible. He reminded His people that He listens, acts, and holds all authority.

This is both comfort and a challenge because, in His sovereignty, evil will not have the last word and inactivity and apathy can't delay His plans. We must keep our eyes on what He has spoken. Whether we see it or not, a new day has begun, and God is faithful to bring His Word to pass.

Chapter 8

Stand With Me, Stands Against Me

May 18, 2021

THIS WORD IS DIRECT, urgent, and uncompromising. God is talking to the church yet again about getting on His side and He reminds us, once again, that neutrality is not an option. We cannot stand silent in the face of deception or else we are conceding ground to the enemy. If judgment begins with the house of God (1 Peter 4:17), we must live soberly.

We are always called to choose, even though we're already His people. We are called to choose life or death, blessings or curses, faithfulness or compromise (Deuteronomy 30:19). This word carries the theme of there being a dividing line within the church. He assures those who have been faithful, rebukes those who have given in to the enemy's lies and calls all to return to His Word.

- *The Message* -

"The time is almost up for the church, My body, to honor Me and stand with Me. Those who did and are, great rewards await you. For those who did not and led people away in faith and conceded—judgment and indignation (Exodus 32). I love you and I am not throwing you away, but you will realize the depth of your error!"

. . .

Exodus 32:1-8 recalls a time when Israel created and worshipped a golden calf. The nation's leaders had failed in their responsibility of leading and gave in to the people's demands to have something to worship, allowing them to build a golden calf and turn away from the Lord. In the same way, God is calling out those in the church who compromise truth. Yet even in this correction, the Lord's love is evident: "I love you and I am not throwing you away."

"Those who did not stand in truth but perpetrated a lie or allowed it to go on unchecked and unresisted are the ones I am looking at. Night is almost here for Me to close this out and to bring the dawn. When the first rays are seen in truth, you missed your opportunity, and I will replace your influence with new guards who can believe God for the impossible, who know there is a God in heaven that speaks and shows forth glory in the heavens and on the earth." (Psalms 19; Psalms 148:13)

This section of the word reflects the parable of the ten virgins (Matthew 25:1-13). When the bridegroom returned, some of the virgins were ready with oil in their lamps and others were not. The warning here is clear: those who fail to stand will see their influence replaced by those who are trusting God fully.

"I stand at a crossroad with you, for those in My church who will stand and believe and not remain quiet and those who have laid down their armor and relegated themselves to slavery to the wicked (Matthew 11:12). I call you to stand and believe, to hear My voice over your feelings, over your mind and reasonings. My Word will stand; My Word will be fulfilled according to My desires and not the enemy's (Isaiah 40:6-8). Hear Me now and be rewarded with great treasure; refuse me, and experience great loss (Hebrews 11:6). I, the Lord, have spoken.

Special Note: The Lord is ramping up to overthrow this (bad actors, traitors, and consequentially the 2020 election), just like the enemy is racing to implement all of these "slavery laws" to put us in bondage. God's power is in no comparison to that, but He is releasing His ability to do what must be done.

. . .

Hebrews 11:6 says that without faith, "it is impossible to please God, because anyone who comes to Him must believe that He exists and that He rewards those who earnestly seek Him." Faith and obedience are mandatory to the Lord, not optional, and this word leaves no room for middle ground.

I find that it's interesting to see the change in tone within this message. To the true, genuine believer there is grace. To the unbeliever and those who are supposed to be the real deal...not so much.

Are we really going to allow a bunch of devil worshippers to win when they have zero real authority? God has given the believer power and authority over all the works of the evil one. We do not have to be afraid of him (the enemy). The time for wavering is over, and God is clear: we must either stand with Him or stand against Him.

Chapter 9

They Wanted Chaos

June 5, 2021

THERE IS a tone change in this prophetic word. After the prophetic word given in chapter 8, this word comes across sharper and more judicial. God moves from exercising patience to issuing a stern warning. What the enemy intended for God's people would now return on his own head.

We see this in Scripture. Psalm 7:15-16 declares,

"Whoever digs a hole and scoops it out falls into the pit they have made. The trouble they cause recoils on them; their violence comes down on their own heads."

God is not mocked. What the wicked sow, they will also reap. While they plot chaos, it's this chaos that will consume them. For the righteous, however, this word is one of hope, mercy, and favor.

- *The Message* -

"They are going to get exactly what they wanted–chaos in their own lives! What they plan to do with us is being brought down on their own heads. Not one of them will escape—no more deals after the announcement!" (Psalms 7:15)

. . .

God has had a history of turning the enemy's schemes back on him. Haman, who built the gallows for Mordecai in Ester 7:10, was hanged on it himself. Likewise, Pharaoh, who drowned Hebrew boys in the Nile, perished in the Red Sea (Exodus 14:28). Wicked plots always collapse under God's justice.

"You have had your time, now it's our turn. And you think Jesus the Lord was a little passive lamb to curse, rail at, to belittle and cast aside with disdain! (Revelation 5:5) Wrong! Witness now the Lion of the Tribe of Judah in glorious power and might to rule, and this is not even the real end yet! Woe to the rest of you when it is, if you refuse His leadership and refuse to repent."

Revelation 5:5 presents Jesus as both the Lamb who was slain and the Lion of Judah who conquers. The world may say what they want about Him, but this prophetic word reminds us that His return as Judge and King will silence every scoffer.

"God is God and there is no other. He rules, He chastises the nations, He brings forth water from a rock! No one is like Him, no one is His equal, no one dares to overthrow Him!" (Exodus 17:1-7; Psalms 94:10)

In Exodus 17:1-6, we see God bringing water forth from a rock to provide for His people. He is sovereign and has the power to supply. Psalms 94:10 asks, "Does He who disciplines the nations not punish? Does He who teaches mankind lack knowledge?"

The prophetic declaration is simple: there is no one equal to God. He disciplines nations, provides for His own, and stands unchallenged.

"For the godly, the meek, the chaste, humble, the loving of God and a defender of His Ways—loving kindness and mercy to you, graciousness, and favor abound to

you! Lift your heads, lift your hearts and receive what God has in store for you! (Psalms 5:12) He lives, He is Lord, He is Savior, He is the King!"

The word closes with a sharp contrast. While the wicked inherit chaos, the righteous inherit blessing. It's a stark warning to the evil ones and their plans. He is not just going to allow unchecked wickedness forever, and we are not just waiting for judgment after people die. Even as God brings down the proud, He raises up His faithful ones with mercy, grace, and protection.

Chapter 10

Who Do You Say I AM?

July 1, 2021

SOME WORDS COME AS DECLARATIONS, others as visions, and others come as continuations of previous messages. This word is one of those updates. It has to do with what He's doing now, what He's already done, and what He's still bringing to pass.

The central question in this word is, "Who do you say I AM?" This is the same question Jesus asked His disciples in Matthew 16:15. It's a question of both spiritual perception and trust in His ability. Will the church declare Christ boldly or cower in silence while wickedness multiplies around them?

Take your time and absorb the context considering the current conditions in America.

- *The Message* -

"Those who committed suicide as they saw the utter hopelessness of the situation in the flesh, the blood of those people is on the hands of those who have committed this fraud and deceit (Genesis 4:10).

Kevin Winkler

It is also partly on some of the churches and ministries of those who threw out the Holy Spirit's leading and decided to follow after man's thoughts (Mark 7:13).

Woe to them for this grievous error."

Here, God points to the devastating consequences of spiritual negligence. In Genesis 4:10, we see Abel's blood crying out from the ground, and here, too, the cries of the innocent blood reach God's ears. Mark 7:13 warns of nullifying God's Word for human traditions. This warning applies directly to churches and leaders who set aside the Spirit's wisdom and guidance and allow worldly reasoning to triumph.

"God is raising new guards for this new era who will tell the people the truth even if it is not popular. There is hope in the Lord, but not for the unrepentant wicked person who practices evil. Nor is it for those who support, defend and condone the practice of wickedness. This includes those who support ministry and others who are okay with it"(Proverbs 24:20).

Proverbs 24:20 reminds us that evildoers have no hope, and "the lamp of the wicked will be snuffed out." God makes it clear that while He is the God of hope and hope abounds with Him, those who are unrepentant and persist in doing evil will not abound in hope. He will raise up "new guards," those with bold voices, who will speak truth without fear.

"Where is your backbone, O' My Church? Who bewitched you? How cowardly have you become (Galatians 3:1-9).

How complacent are your ways?

Stand and speak, stand and share, stand and do not be silent in this face of evil" *(Romans 12:9).*

Romans 12:9 states, "Love must be sincere. Hate what is evil; cling to what is good." It reminds us that complacency is not neutral. This is a timeless principle, from biblical times to the times we live in. God calls His people to courage and not cowardice.

"I, the Lord, have spoken.

What more do you need? Will you not listen, will you not heed? Will only a few enjoy the rich rewards of God? Yes, I said rewards! Do you not yet understand, is this too difficult for you to comprehend? (Psalms 35).

You shall not mock those whom I establish in My favor, when they stood and you sat idly by. There are even those who do not belong to Me yet who have stood on the side of truth. What excuses can you render to Me? What will you say when I call you to account? 'I did not know?'

You knew all right!

My Spirit gave you time to see the wickedness, to be exposed to pure evil. I allowed you this time to see what it will be like if I do not intercede.

Yet I have chosen not to allow this nation to fall at this time in human history. I have chosen for the sake of My elect, to lift her back up (Proverbs 11:10-11).

It was I who allowed this exposure of corruption to take place. Did I not tell you this ahead of time? Did I not say the world would be shaken—your world? (Psalms 37)

Who do you say I Am?

Who do you think I Am?

A stone carved to look like a man or beast of the earth?

I Am He who lives forever! Who is like Me?

Yet you still will not believe. I told you, My church, that it was for you, to wake you up, to give you an opportunity to be in on My plan in the world.

I told you your time was almost up to repent, before I will judge.

I will bless whom I will bless. I will honor whom I will honor. I will reward whom I will reward. I will give to whom I will give (Romans 9:18).

Come now and say, "The Lord is my Rock, the Lord is my God!" (Psalms 18:2)

I, the Lord have spoken to My servant—take heed and do not dare discount this message as some have done."

Some of the language in this word reads like a rebuke to the church. As members of the body of Christ, it's up to us to speak up when we see people, notably our own fellow brothers and sisters, not adhering to truth. God desires for His people to boldly and publicly confess His lordship.

This message makes it clear that we must be careful. We have to do our research when it comes to who we support in ministry because sometimes, we are unknowingly supporting activities that directly violate God's written Word. This would include ministries and churches that support anti-biblical positions, such as those that agree with the LGBTQ lifestyle. God is not okay with us supporting and defending people who oppose His standards of morality. This would be a violation of love, because these activities, without repentance, have eternal consequences.

Jesus died to save us from sin, which is why I believe this prophetic word pierces with such urgency. The body of Christ is called out of compromise and into courage. And even now, He promises to lift up the nation for the sake of the elect.

Chapter 11

Almost Over–Keep Up the Faith

August 20, 2021

AT ABOUT MID-2021, I asked the Lord if He had another word for what was going on in our country and in the world. He answered by reminding me of something crucial: He does not change His mind.

In fact, what He put in my heart was this:

- The Message -

What has He already said, what has He already spoken? He does not change His mind like we do, and He's not fickle in His feelings about things. What He says He's going to do is what He's going to do.

I felt strongly that this word was for and about the current state of the United States and the fraud, deceit, and evil plans of the wicked to enslave this great nation and its people. However, it also extends to the rest of the world.

This word is not something new, but rather a "pointing back" to what He'd already said. He also specifically put Psalms 64 and 68 on my heart, as they both speak about Israel's enemies and mirror the events we saw shaping our world at the time.

"God is [already] beginning to arise, and His enemies to scatter; let them also who hate Him flee before Him!

As smoke is driven away, so drive them away; as wax melts before the fire, so let the wicked perish before the presence of God.

But let the [uncompromisingly] righteous be glad; let them be in high spirits and glory before God, yes, let them [jubilantly] rejoice!

Sing to God, sing praises to His name, cast up a highway for Him Who rides through the deserts—His name is the Lord—be in high spirits and glory before Him!" (Psalm 68:1-4 [AMPC])

This psalm opens by depicting God on the move. He's scattering enemies, melting the wicked, and lifting up the righteous in joy. His actions are decisive and visible, and just as He rose to defend Israel, He arises today to defend His people.

"Hear my voice, O God, in my complaint; guard and preserve my life from the terror of the enemy.

Hide me from the secret counsel and conspiracy of the ungodly, from the scheming of evildoers,

Who whet their tongues like a sword, who aim venomous words like arrows,

Who shoot from ambush at the blameless man; suddenly do they shoot at him, without self-reproach or fear.

They encourage themselves in an evil purpose, they talk of laying snares secretly; they say, Who will discover us?

They think out acts of injustice and say, We have accomplished a well-devised thing! For the inward thought of each one [is unsearchable] and his heart is deep.

But God will shoot an unexpected arrow at them; and suddenly shall they be wounded.

And they will be made to stumble, their own tongues turning against them; all who gaze upon them will shake their heads and flee away.

And all men shall [reverently] fear and be in awe; and they will declare the work of God, for they will wisely consider and acknowledge that it is His doing.

The [uncompromisingly] righteous shall be glad in the Lord and shall trust and take refuge in Him; and all the upright in heart shall glory and offer praise." (Psalms 64:1-10 [AMPC])

This psalm shows the wicked scheming in hidden places, confident that no one will expose them. But we see divine reversal: even if they feel they are succeeding in wickedness, God Himself will shoot His arrow, and their own words will undo them.

We've seen this over and again in biblical history. Pharaoh pursued the Israelites, and it ended in his own destruction (Exodus 14:28). Haman's schemes destroyed him (Esther 7:10), and Daniel's enemies were thrown into the very lion's den they intended for him (Daniel 6:24).

This word, again, is less of a new revelation and more of a reminder that God has already spoken. With His Word as the anchor, He encourages us to keep the faith.

Chapter 12

A Vision: The Highway

September 21, 2021

THIS WORD actually came as a vision. Sometimes, God not only shows you a picture of something, but also downloads its interpretation directly to your heart.

Throughout Scripture, God has used the imagery of roads and highways to convey His plans and promises. Isaiah 35:8 speaks of a "highway...called the Way of Holiness; it will be for those who walk on that Way." Similarly, Isaiah 40:3 says, "In the wilderness prepare the way for the Lord; make straight in the desert a highway for our God." This depicts both the direction and the preparation God provides for His people.

This vision is encouraging. God has set before His people a wide, open path to destiny that's free from obstruction yet requires courage to walk when others hesitate.

- *The Message* -

I saw a highway before us. This highway was multiple lanes wide, and the lanes were all going in the same direction. This highway was five, maybe even six lanes wide heading into the distance. This highway was wide and open; it was straight and smooth. As I looked down this highway it was going into the distance as far as I can see, and in the distance was light like the light of the setting or the rising of the sun at about 10 a.m. It was not orange or red, but the light of day and was bright.

The Lord was showing us this beautiful wide open space that was straight before us, straight into our destiny, but there weren't a lot of people on it at all. I felt like it was actually quite empty, void of traffic, but it was given before us and I believe that is a highway that God has put us on—that's not restrictive, but there is a lot of room to maneuver in the direction God wants us to go (Isaiah 35:8-10).

(Special Note: I think the vision of it being void of a lot of traffic really represented to me there wasn't a lot of leadership, churches or ministries heading in this direction. I don't think this represents God's work for other people through this ministry. I think we're heading in this way and we can't worry about how many other churches and ministries or leaders are heading this way on this highway. We just have to do what He's called us to do and not worry about what other people are doing.)

When Elijah felt alone, God reminded him that there were 7,000 other prophets He'd reserved who had not bowed down to Baal (1 Kings 19:18). Likewise, Paul told the Galatians, "Each one should test their own actions...for each one should carry their own load" (Galatians 6:4-5). Our call is to stay faithful to the path God has given each of us, regardless of what others are doing or how many people are staying on their own path.

He reminded me of a vision from a previous word where He showed me His altar and in front of His altar were all these things–pieces of equipment, ability, all kinds of items that we might need or need to use in our life and they were all available for the taking, all available to use for whatever endeavor we needed. I was reminded that all we have to do is go get what we need from Him. That He's provided everything for our enjoyment, but also everything to live a godly life (1 Timothy 6:17).

All this that we are given access to is in the service of the King. He wants us to depend on His ability, which is His grace. It empowers us to accomplish things.

The things He wants us to accomplish He has already shared in their various forms but would like us to believe Him that it will come to pass. We're going to need Him and we're going to need His grace to see them fulfilled.

I have already said, be of good cheer. He has already overcome the world for us. Don't ever hesitate to ask for help, to be dependent on Him. Never feel like He is not wanting to hear from you. He has done all this for you; to have you, to keep you. He says to come to Him, don't hold back, don't be afraid of His rejection of you, if you are trying, keep working on it—keep getting up (John 16:33; Matthew 11:28-30).

Here, He blends encouragement with invitation. In John 16:33, Jesus tells us that He has already overcome the world, while Matthew 11:28-30 reminds us to come to Him to receive rest. God abundantly provides and He makes His presence accessible, but He tells us to continue to approach "the throne of grace, where we find grace and mercy to help in time of need" (Hebrews 4:16).

God is giving us a lot of room. He is not restricting our call or movement. He wants us to dream and believe and ask; to take steps while allowing His Spirit to open up to us the impossible!

This is our future. The Lord, He wants us to have it now and not to delay, not to be afraid to take the steps. We are not to try to do it all by ourselves, but to allow Him to help us. That's His joy, that's His love, that's His heart to be there to see us prosper in everything we do.

His hand is upon us and is surrounding us. His hand is mighty, to bring down and destroy every hindering spirit, every spirit of delay, every spirit of depression, every spirit of bondage, every spirit of strongholds. He can do the impossible and He wants to do the impossible for us, for you, for me. This is the message.

As far as His movement in the world, for the world as a whole, not just for the United States of America.

What He is doing is not a hard thing, but an easy thing for Him. To man it's complicated, to man it seems impossible, but to the Lord God, nothing is impossible. And He is opening wide His victory, and it is great, and it is grand, and it is available for everyone on earth to partake of. The victories of God are truly grand, phenomenal, and wondrous.

God was not going to let us be turned over to these people. It wasn't in His heart for us to be given over to these people. It was in His heart for them to repent and come to the saving knowledge of Jesus Christ and for them to come to understand that there is a God in heaven who rules over the nations.

But alas, not everyone would listen and not everyone would repent and not everyone would turn, even when they know and knew that God was trying to have mercy upon them and reach them—they rejected it, rejected His grace, rejected His hand of deliverance for their own life and now the Lord is bringing this to a conclusion. He is restoring the United States to even greater levels then it was before. He is bringing the rest of the world along with it. These other countries and people will be wiser for the wear in how they are relating to who they have in charge.

This reminds us of Daniel 2:21: "He changes times and seasons; He deposes kings and raises up others." God truly rules over the nations. He offers mercy and deliverance, but He brings judgment when mercy is rejected.

The Lord God in one fell swoop will release His great power and in a single day bring great victories to the people... There is one last moment, for those who don't want to believe in His ability, to get in on this, to believe that God can and will deliver the country and the world from this wicked plan.

God is going to do this and for those who prayed for His help, for those who believed Him that He could, for those who, even if they had bouts of doubt, would stand their ground and believe anyway, for those who would listen to the prophets and others who were bringing the news of heaven and believed, for those who did not give up on God and kept crying out to Him with tears and with groanings, He will completely vindicate you.

"I am the Lord and there is no other. I stretched out the heavens and founded the earth upon the seas. I created life from nothing, calling everything into being that was made. I am the Lord, and I have spoken."

. . .

It's amazing to look back, in hindsight, and see what the Lord has already done and what He's doing. When He said, "The Lord God in one fell swoop will release His great power and in a single day bring great victories to the people," we can recognize where He caused what seemed impossible to come to pass.

God is assuring vindication for the faithful. This prophetic word closes with God's self-revelation as both the Creator and Sustainer. He is the One who spoke the world into being and He will bring His promises to completion.

Chapter 13

A Vision: The Whirlwind

October 1, 2021

ONCE AGAIN, the Lord spoke here through a vision, providing understanding and insight along with it. This time, it was a powerful whirlwind stretching from earth to heaven. This whirlwind was not meant for the righteous, but for the wicked.

We see whirlwinds used in Scripture as symbols of God's judgment and cleansing. Jeremiah 23:19 says, "The storm of the Lord will burst out in wrath, a whirlwind swirling down on the heads of the wicked." What terrifies the wicked can be a sign of mercy to those who are righteous.

- The Message -

Standing before me, turning and roaring, is a massive whirlwind. It is churning and spinning with great force. It is filled with debris and is brown in color as it whips around in its circling. As I stand before my God, speaking to Him the whirlwind comes close to me, right before my face, as I look straight up, this towering tornado stretches to the heights of heaven. It spins, it moves to the left and to the right slowly coming close to me—without touching me.

I was speaking to the Lord God Most High, my Father. To me the whirlwind was not scary; I know it is sent to wipe away and scour the land of wickedness–to leave for me, for us, a clean foundation. I know this tornadic wind is not for me or us, those living inside God's will, but those who are to be wiped away. For us, it is God's help and mercy; to them, it is utter destruction (Exodus 14:10-25).

In Exodus 14, God used the Red Sea as a source of both salvation and judgment. It was salvation for the Israelites, but judgment for Pharaoh's army. The whirlwind in this prophetic word carries the same dual meaning; destruction for the wicked, deliverance for those living in God's will.

I pray for those political leaders to turn to God. I speak with my God that I do not want them to go to hell, I so want them to repent. But even if their lives are to be ruined and destroyed, to be brought down to the gutters in the street, never to rise again, O' that they should then, even then, look up to God and reach for Him and tell Him they are sorry, to receive His gracious forgiveness (1 Timothy 2:1-4).

The whirlwind is here for them, not for us.

Save them, O' Lord, and rescue us.

The angelic hosts, the mighty ones of God are in position. They are in place and are awaiting the command of God, as His Spirit is still working through the hearts and lives of men in mercy.

This tornado will not cease until it finishes its cleansing.

I, the Lord, have shared this vision. I, the Lord, have spoken with My servant and friend.

You would think that seeing something like this in the Spirit would be frightening. However, when you know God and have fellowship with Him, you know there's nothing to be afraid of.

This word also echoes passages like Psalm 91, where God promises to protect His people even when they're surrounded by disaster. He says in verse seven, "A thousand may fall at your side, ten thousand at your right hand, but it will not come near you." Ultimately, the whirlwind reminds us that God is not passive when it comes to evil. He will not hesitate to cleanse, vindicate His people, and establish them on a renewed foundation.

Part Three

2022 | The Coming Dawn

Section Notes

As you have witnessed. God has plans. They will come to pass as He has said. In this section the tone is changing. See if you can identify why and how.

Chapter 14

The Gates of Hell Have Not Prevailed

January 31, 2022

THIS PROPHETIC WORD may be one of my favorites. God reveals that He's not turning His true followers over to their enemy, but rather, that He loves us and wants us all to walk in our God-given authority. The very title itself echoes Jesus' promise in Matthew 16:18, where He says that He would build His church, "and the gates of hell shall not prevail against it." It's a reminder that no scheme of the enemy and no earthly power can overcome the church that Christ is building.

- *The Message* -

My God what do you say? What do you declare?

"O' My People whom I have chosen, who have declared their allegiance to Me, I am Your God and there is no other" (Isaiah 41:10).

Isaiah 41:10 reminds us not to fear because God is with us. It is comforting when God reassures His people of His presence and sovereignty!

. . .

"What has Your Maker declared? What have I put forth to you? How have I failed you? Who can know what I am doing from beginning to the end? (Hebrews 13:5; Deuteronomy 31:8)

Does the world think so little of what God says? Do its inhabitants not understand or have simply forgotten it was I who created all things by My great power and might—I said, and it was. I spoke and things were so" (Psalms 33:9).

Psalms 33:9 declares, "He spoke, and it came to be; He commanded, and it stood firm." Though the world may dismiss and ignore God's Word, creation itself testifies that Jesus by His word sustains all things.

"Why do you put such little importance on My Word? Who do you know that can actually stop Me from fulfilling My desires and plans? What power is there besides Me to accomplish that? Don't believe false power rooted in the enemy. Don't believe your own eyes that try to perceive something that may not be there—believe God's voice in your inner man. He gives the ability to discern the truth. Please, listen to Me. I will show you signs and wonders, awesome signs on the earth. I will allow you to see my hand moving and to discern that indeed, it is Me. But the deceiver wants to show false signs of power (Isaiah 14:27, 43:13; Revelation 13:13-14; Jeremiah 33:3).

I the Lord say, be not afraid, but be of good cheer. Speak your faith! Take your stand. I am with you and my remnant. I love those who love Me. I am for those who are for Me. I stand in contrast to the lies of the enemy. Who does he think he is? He assumes to take My throne and has failed. And he will be no more (Isaiah 14:12-15; Revelation 12:4; Isaiah 14:13).

I, the Lord, have spoken."

Satan's lies are always temporary and attempt to distract us from what God has already said. God's Word, however, is eternal. This word is a rallying cry that the gates of hell have not prevailed and they never will. The church is not left powerless, even in the midst of circumstances that don't reflect His Word. The final word is and always will be: "I, the Lord, have spoken."

Chapter 15

My Power an Might Shall be Known

February 14, 2022

WHEN GOD SPEAKS a word more than once, we need to pay attention because this indicates that He wants us to take that word seriously. This word was originally given in early 2022 and released again in May 2023. The theme is unmistakable: God will not ignore wickedness forever. His mercy and patience have limits, and when people persist in rejecting Him, He eventually responds in judgment.

We see this pattern in Scripture. In the book of Judges, we see the Israelites in a cycle of sinning against God, receiving judgment, and crying out to Him for help. In response, He has mercy on them by raising up a judge to deal with their enemies. When they continued to sin and pushed beyond the boundaries of God's mercy again, the cycle would continue, and God would once again bring judgment.

- *The Message* -

God is not playing around as it relates to evil and the wicked schemes concocted and implemented by evil men. The wrath of God is their lot now.

"They chose a path that was not My will. They wanted nothing to do with Me or righteousness. I have spoken, I have warned, I have held out My hand. They wanted to go on in their wickedness."

God here describes the persistence of the wicked. Proverbs 29:1 warns us that "whoever remains stiff-necked after many rebukes will suddenly be destroyed–without remedy." God's offer of mercy had been extended, but their refusal to respond brought wrath instead.

"They make sport of their folly. Even after they can see the warning signs of impending judgment and know full well their plans will ultimately fail and come to naught by My power, yet they persist! They see the people arising, they see My hand unraveling their schemes, and they go on to their destruction.

I, the Lord, have spoken from My heavenly dwelling place. I have commanded, and it shall be carried out. My plan shall stand," says the Lord of Hosts. "My ways shall be extended to all the earth.

My power and might shall be known. Woe to the inhabitants of the earth who refuse My hand, My counsel, and My mercy. Where will you hide? To whom will you run in the day of calamity? What can you offer Me to relent? I am the Almighty whom you turn your heels against."

The rhetorical questions here mirror those in Hosea 13:9, which states, "You are destroyed, Israel, because you are against me, against your Helper." God was Israel's refuge and is ours as well, and to reject His mercy is to choose calamity.

"For My faithful ones who continue to love and want My hand, YOU HAVE IT! I shall raise you up and no one shall bring you down anymore. Your name will be great in the earth as my representatives. Your heart shall be renewed and soar far above their calamity. Your life is in My hands and shall remain. I am yours and you are Mine; ask what you will and see Me answer you! I love you. I am Your God! Continue in My ways and see Me all around you.

I, the Lord, have spoken!"

This promise parallels John 15:7, which says that if God's words remain in us, we can ask whatever we wish and it will be done for us. We are not left to fend for ourselves. While the wicked face wrath, the faithful receive renewal and an intimate assurance of God's love.

Chapter 16

The Word of God

AT FIRST GLANCE, this prophetic word seemed like it addressed the Canadian trucker convoy that took place during the COVID-19 lockdowns. Yet like many of the other prophetic words, both in this book and the Bible, it is a double-reference prophecy that transcends one single event. It speaks to a moment while also carrying a future-oriented application.

God gives second chances, which means He sometimes shakes nations to wake them up. He calls His people to open their eyes, recognize deception, and align themselves with His Word. Ephesians 5:14 tells us, "Wake up, sleeper, rise from the dead, and Christ will shine on you."

- The Message -

God is giving you another shot at it. He is giving you another chance. He is not abandoning you. This had to hurt a bit to help those who were slow to respond. Many people, your citizens, pay no mind to the political area of their lives. They ate whatever they were given with eyes half-closed. God needed you to see what your enemy had been doing, the schemes he had been up to...and no, I'm not talking about the flesh and blood enemy. I am talking about the enemy of your souls. That one is allowed to work when we do not stand. Yes, he works through flesh and blood—anyone he can persuade. Silver and gold is his chief persuader.

The opening to this prophetic word reminds us of Paul's words in Ephesians 6:12:

"Our struggle is not against flesh and blood, but against the rulers, against the authorities, against the powers of this dark world and against the spiritual forces of evil in the heavenly realms."

We see other examples throughout Scripture of God giving His people another chance. In Jonah 3:4, we see Him giving Nineveh forty days to repent. Judgment was coming to them, but even so, He desired to show them mercy. Likewise, Israel was repeatedly given opportunities to turn back to Him. He gave them centuries (you read that right) to repent, and when they refused, He finally turned them over to their enemies.

The people need to be awake and watchful going forward to whom you will cast your vote for. Even Satan masquerades "like" an angel of light. Some of these folk's "talk" fancy, persuasively and seem like "good" guys, but their heart is not right (2 Corinthians 11:14).

You cannot separate morality from secularism. Morality comes from a higher authority! And that Authority has written His laws on every human's heart. Those who have rejected that or have not submitted to that are under the control of the enemy (Romans 2:14-16; 1 John 5:19).

Stop listening to their talk and examine their actions. You will know them by their fruit! (Matthew 7:16)

Pick better fruit and reject these rotten ones for now on. Stop being deceived by their elegant speech!

Second Corinthians 11:4 tells us that Satan masquerades as an "angel of light." Appearances can be deceiving, and persuasive speech can mask corruption. Jesus even cautioned His disciples in Matthew 24:24 that false messiahs and false prophets would appear to "deceive, if possible, even the elect." This is why we must be filled with God's Word!

We cannot sit back, close our eyes, and just allow things to take place. This prophetic word calls us to measure leaders and influencers not by their charisma, promises, or polished speech, but by their actions. The Word of God is the plumbline and we must measure everything, including politics, culture, and personal choices, against it. If we stand against the enemy, in Jesus' name, we can put a stop to a lot of nonsense before it ever gets started!

Chapter 17

The President's Pardon

April 7, 2022

THIS MESSAGE IS one of the clearest examples of the prophetic reaching into the future. God reveals events before they happen so His people can endure the waiting, so unbelievers can see that He is sovereign, and so the wicked can turn from their sins.

I had no idea that this word would take over two-and-a-half years to come to pass. This aligns with Amos 3:7, which tells us that the Lord does nothing without revealing His plans to His servants. In this word, we see leaders confronted with their arrogance, comfort for God's people, and a charge to His "appointed one," the president, to act responsibly and with justice.

- The Message -

"I, the Lord, have spoken of My intent at this hour in history.

I have warned the world, and those who have betrayed Me, of what I would do. I have been watching and waiting for repentance for a heart change but see none. Therefore, I, the Lord, command execution of my plan and purposes. I, the Lord, am merciful to those who repent, to those who ask for help, even if they are in the wrong. But to those who are intent on fulfilling their evil designs—I Am a raging fire that will consume" (Revelation; Hebrews 4:24; Deuteronomy 4:2).

This is the ever-present tension of God's nature that we've continued to see throughout this book a mixture of mercy and judgment. He waits for repentance, but when there is none, judgment comes.

"Why is it that you wanted My judgment, O' you leaders of the nations? Why is it you would not yield to Me and do what was right in My sight? Did you really believe that I would not act? Did you deceive yourselves that I am powerless, just an imagination of the religious? I came to give life, not death, hope, not defeat—but you wanted none of it" (Deuteronomy 6:18; Philippians 2:13; Colossians 1:16-17)

Here, God questions the arrogance of rulers who dismiss Him. Deuteronomy 6:18 commands leaders to do what is right in the Lord's sight. To reject Him is to reject life itself.

"See now what I will do before your very eyes. As clearly as the sun is seen you will see (Psalms 37:6).

I will not allow these things to go on and continue. I Am not one who lies or pretends. I speak the truth for all to hear (Numbers 32:19; Titus 1:2; Hebrews, 6:18).

To My President: there is no pardon to the wicked, to the arrogant, to the fearful. They all heard, they all knew, they all went on their way, rejecting My counsel. You shall deal with them as the enemies of God! They will be required to seek My face for solace, I Am He and He alone who shall give it, and by no other shall it come. I waited patiently, enduringly, but that time is now over (Romans 13:1-5).

Fix your eyes on My plan and fulfill your calling as My appointed to exact vengeance for Me (Romans 13:4])

. . .

Romans 13:1-5 shows us that governing authorities are established by God. In fact, this passage tells us that a government is "God's servant, an agent of wrath to bring punishment on the wrongdoer" (Romans 13:4). Here, God addresses His "president," charging him to act with justice against the wicked.

"I have heard your cry, My beloved children. I have seen and indeed know your endurance and that your hope is almost gone. Like an anointing oil poured onto the top of your head, that drips onto your body and soaks into your clothes, is My refreshing of your soul before Me. I will redeem and deliver My people from the contempt of My ways! (Psalms 23)

To you My love is given. To you are My plans established; with you are they confirmed. Arise and go forth, to fill your calling and execute justice in the land.

I, the Lord, have spoken."

In Psalm 23, David refers to the Lord anointing his head with oil. This imagery in this word of oil soaking through the body and clothing paints a picture of deep renewal. For a weary people, He is promising not just survival but refreshing and vindication.

This word shows God's sovereignty over leaders, nations, and even history itself. To the wicked and unrepentant, there is a guarantee of judgment. To His appointed leader, the call is to act with courage and make sure justice is executed. Lastly, to His people, He promises relief, refreshing, and vindication. The gates of hell will not prevail, no matter what we see. God promises His sovereignty over the affairs of men!

Chapter 18

The Supremacy of the Court Belongs to Me

April 7, 2022

THROUGHOUT SCRIPTURE, God makes it clear that justice ultimately belongs to Him. He raises up leaders and brings them down and turns the hearts of kings like water in His hand (Daniel 2:21; Proverbs 21:1). Likewise, when human systems exalt evil, He confronts them (Psalm 2; Isaiah 5:20).

God knows people's fruit. We, likewise, need to be discerning and not just hear what people say, but look at what they are actually doing. This word speaks straight into this reality. Even when human courts and judicial systems reward unrighteousness, God Himself will assert jurisdiction. Our refuge is not in an institution or even a government, but in a God who judges righteously.

- *The Message* -

"They put a vile one on the Supreme Court of the land, thinking that is the way to be saved.

I Am NOT a respecter of persons. Would this stop Me? I gave the breath of life, and I can also take it away. I call things that are not as though they were (Romans 4:17).

Where is your sanctuary, where is your hiding place, where is your confidence? In man? I laugh at your utter contempt for Me. The land belongs to Me. The seas belong to Me, the skies belong to Me, and so does divine judgment. This will be short-lived and shall not stand as it is not of Me!

The perpetrators are in for a big surprise as I reveal my plans and purposes (Psalm 94).

I, the Lord, have spoken!"

This word references "a vile one on the Supreme Court." This has happened before in Scripture; when seats of judgment are twisted, God called it out. In fact, Psalm 94:20 tells us "Shall the throne of iniquity have fellowship with you, which frames mischief by a law?" Titles will not shield anyone from His verdict.

Prophetic Update:

By June of 2025 (at the publishing of this book), we had already discovered that the autopen was used for many of the previous presidential documents that were signed during that time. Everything signed with that device, without the president's permission and authority, is void. What would happen if the 2020 election were actually proven to be a fraud? What would happen to laws that were signed into effect? What about the damage that was done by the executive orders put into place at that time? Was the Biden Administration an illegitimate Presidency?

Our true shelter is in the secret place of the Most High (Psalm 91:1). This word re-centers the church and helps us ask ourselves, "Where is our confidence? How do we discern? What do we do?" If a court decision is not in alignment with His Word, it will not stand. Our role is to stay under His covering, keep our hearts centered on Him, and contend in prayer. He is the Lord, and He will not fail us.

Chapter 19

The New Era of the Church

April 21, 2022

GOD IS NOT FINISHED with His church. In fact, He is calling the church into a new era. This will be a season that looks like both purging and renewal. Jesus declared in John 15:2 that "every branch that bears fruit He prunes, that it may bear more fruit."

Throughout history, the church has faced times of refining. God has always used refining to purify and empower His bride. For instance, the Reformation and revivals of past centuries served to shake off corruption and reignite holiness, prayer, and evangelism.

In this season, God was stripping away what was unnecessary and emphasizing what was essential. We had to ask ourselves, "Is the corporate structure or business of churches being altered? If so, what is God shifting and how must we respond?"

Kevin Winkler

- *The Message* -

"What does God want to do in this new era of the church?

There is a victorious church God is raising up. The church has been pruned and is undergoing a purging. Many unnecessary things are being taken away. Many essentials are being emphasized.

God's desire is for His bride to be radiant, not comparable to any other. No religion or cult should look like Her in power.

The bride, the church, should be pure, loving, and genuine, a worthy adversary to the kingdom of darkness" (Ephesians 5:26-27; Revelations 19:7).

Paul wrote that Christ loved the church and gave Himself up for her to cleanse her (Ephesians 5:26-27). Here, the Lord appears to be emphasizing that His bride is to be radiant, pure, and full of His power. The culmination of that vision is Revelation 19:7, which says that "The wedding of the Lamb has come, and His bride has made herself ready."

The Bride should enjoy all of the rightful benefits of her position and relationship with God. We are not supposed to think lightly of God's care and blessings to her. She should not be treated by God like the rest of the world who is not His betrothed. God is God of all; He rules over the nations, the earth and the fullness are His, but not everyone wants to be His. Therefore, He does not consider them His own, but strangers and outcasts from His wonderful presence—workers of iniquity, rebellious without cause, mere spectators of God's goodness and kindness —though He Himself traded His life for theirs to cleanse them and to welcome them into life and faith. But alas, they still want Him not.

This section reminds us of John 1:12-13. God tells us that to all who received and believed in His name, "He gave them the right to become children of God." Scripture is clear that not everyone is a child of God. That title is only reserved for those who belong to Christ.

The distinction here is clear: God rules over creation, but His favor and intimacy belong only to His bride.

. . .

"I want them, but they don't want Me," says the Lord. "My kindness and slowness to anger should not be construed as my favor or my approval, but much patience for repentance (Psalms 47:8; John 1:12-13, 3:16 – 21; 1 Timothy 2:4).

My favor and approval is to My bride to true and faithful ones, who want to error no more.

Follow Me and see My plans for you!

I, the Lord, have spoken."

The Lord has placed a lot of emphasis on His bride. He is speaking exclusively about her having His favor, and He does treat her differently–as it should be. He calls us, the bride of Christ, to follow Him into a new era where the church is being pruned, empowered, and prepared to stand against darkness.

Chapter 20

The Great Awakening

July 20, 2022

THROUGHOUT HISTORY, God has opened people's eyes who once walked in darkness and caused them to see His truth clearly. We see this happen, for instance, during the Great Awakening movements that brought people to a place of repentance and sparked revival in entire regions.

This prophetic word hints at a time to come when the same thing would happen, but on an even greater level. This will not only be spiritual, but a societal awakening that unmasks deception and causes those who oppose truth to see reality. God makes them very aware of the enemy's plans so that even those who once were under the influence of deception can see it for what it is.

- The Message -

"There are powerful people behind the scenes working. They know, and they can see. They were already aware of what these people wanted to do. And in many ways were ready, but the people (the public) were not ready to do what must be done. But they are ready and getting ready by the day. Even the most staunch supporter of the deception, the other side, are having their eyes opened to the

"real" plan and agenda, and it is horrifying. They will become allies instead of enemies–apostates" (Luke 8:17; Romans 8:28).

This word reveals that God is both preparing people behind-the-scenes and is opening people's eyes to deception. This should reassure us that God is not caught off-guard. He has people in places (even if we don't know they're there), He is opening eyes (even if we can't see it), and He's weaving things together for the good of His people (even if it looks grim). Even though this word was released to me in 2022, this was already happening then and is happening to an even greater degree today.

Chapter 21

It's Raining: God Bless America

August 11, 2022

THIS MESSAGE IS one of encouragement and renewal. God is the one who waters us and helps us grow in godliness. In Scripture, rain is often a metaphor for God's blessing, restoration, and the outpouring of His Holy Spirit.

Deuteronomy 32:2 says, "Let my teaching fall like rain and My Words descend like dew, like showers on new grass, like abundant rain on tender plants." As you read this wonderful message of hope, allow God to water your own soul. Although judgment is real for those who reject Him, He is pouring out His Spirit and blessing those who turn to Him.

- The Message -

"My people are destroyed for a lack of knowledge. So, I gave them knowledge, and many heeded My voice and turned to see. But some did not. They are responsible for their demise (Hosea 4:6).

I called to them, and they refused. I tried to show them, and they would not turn their heads to see. Do you think this is the first time in My history that this has happened? I have dealt with stiff-necked people in the past and I am doing it again" (Proverbs 1:24; Isaiah 66:4; Jeremiah 7:13).

91

. . .

This is a sobering reminder that when people reject knowledge from God, destruction soon follows. Even so, He is shown mercifully calling to His people and inviting them to see the truth. This is consistent with Proverbs 1:24-26, in which "wisdom" is speaking. When we refuse to heed wisdom, wisdom "laughs" when disaster strikes us.

"I AM witness to nations and kingdoms rising and falling from the beginning. It is I who raise up one and bring another down—this is not by chance! It is I; I AM He who governs above the affairs of men (Psalms 75:7).

I have seen the calamity caused by the unrepentant. I am aware of their doings, even those done in secret! Will their plans succeed? Will they be allowed to carry them out to the full? What do you say? Are you listening to Me?" (Exodus 2:23-25)

Scripture contains accounts of secret schemes plotted against God's people. God, here, reminds us that being aware of His sovereignty should cause us to trust Him, not fear Him.

"I the Lord have spoken; I am sending the rain, and rain is beginning to fall. Remember my servant, Elijah? (1 Kings 17) Do you not perceive it? The parched ground of My people is being watered to bring forth abundantly. I shall not let them fall, I am holding them up, My chosen! I am calling forth the increase for and to them!" (1 Corinthians 3:6-8)

Elijah prayed for rain after years of drought (1 Kings 18:41-45). Paul wrote in 1 Corinthians 3:6-8 that one plants, another person waters, but God makes things grow.

"America, America, I, the Lord, formed you. I saw you in utter seclusion, when you were yet unformed. I knitted you together. I shall save you yet for another

season and YOU SHALL SHINE AS A CITY ON A HILL AGAIN!" (Psalms 139:15-16; James 5:15; Matthew 5:14)

In Psalm 139:15-16, God talks about forming us in the womb. Here, God is applying it to the formation of a nation. This is a prophetic reassurance that America will shine again because of God's mercy and His purposes.

"My beloved servants. Lead My people to victory! Lead them to restoration in Me! I care about their lives. I the Lord care, I the Lord have compassion and see their plight and am He who rules! I say what shall be! (Psalms 145:13-14)

Take the rain in my people, take the rain in and flourish...

The wicked who rose up against you shall not stand nor shall they continue. (Deuteronomy 28:7; Isaiah 41:12)

Look up and see, look up and watch My hand as I deliver you and your little ones from the hands of the oppressor (Psalms 119:134).

Take your place and stand! Stand firm. Stand in Me and My strength!

Can you see? Can you hear what the Spirit is speaking?

I AM here!"

These words reflect Deuteronomy 28:7, which says, "The Lord will cause your enemies who rise against you to be defeated." They also reflect Isaiah 41:12: "Those who wage war against you will be as nothing at all." The call is not just to receive the Lord's rain, but to also stand firm in God's strength.

This word also mirrors Psalms 23. The Good Shepherd restores, leads His people beside still waters, and even prepares a table before His people in the presence of His enemies. It warns God's people that those who refuse His call are responsible for their own destruction, and it reflects hope that He is sending the restoring rain. But most of all, it seems to carry a sense of promise for our nation, that America will shine again because of God's sovereign hand.

Chapter 22

A Vision: The Flag

August 10, 2022

GOD COMMUNICATES with us in many ways because He wants all His children to know Him and to hear Him. He speaks through His written Word, by His Spirit, and through prophetic messages, dreams, visions, rewards and gifts. He also speaks through discipline and punishment, supernatural knowledge, the gift of the word of knowledge, and by His audible voice.

For the believer, having God communicate with us should be a normal encounter. We are His children, so it stands to reason that He has to talk to His kids often. What is written in His Word is the most important, but we are not solely limited to Him speaking to us only through His written Word. I believe His idea was not for us to just learn about Him through His Word, but through ongoing communication through the Spirit of God.

- *The Message* -

Tonight (Wednesday August 10, 2022), I went in to do devotionals with my wife and child. As I was praying, I was thanking God for the rain out loud (in reference to the previous prophetic word). As I was giving Him thanks again for the rain that He sent on the land, I had a vision of the American flag in my spirit. It was not the whole flag, but the center part with the red and white stripes.

I know that God is saving this country. I know that He had us wait and be patient for all the pieces of His plan to come together (Psalms 106:13 [AMPC]).

I personally feel as though the attack of the FBI on President Donald Trump's personal residence was an attack on the Lord's appointed. And the attack on him, I felt personally as an attack on me myself. The Lord God is taking action in the physical realm. Don't get me wrong, He has already been at work, but that was the final act.

He gave these people time to repent. He made all of us wait patiently and endure such hopeless feelings, such depression, as we see our country being destroyed by a government that's not legitimate (Acts 17:30; Romans 2:4; 2 Peter 3:9).

Acts 17:30 says that God overlooked ignorance in the past, "but now He commands all people everywhere to repent." We see in Romans 2:4 that His kindness is meant to lead us to repentance because He doesn't want anyone to perish (2 Peter 3:9). He is patient and merciful that we may repent because there is judgment waiting for those who persist in stubbornness.

He has already spoken by the mouth of His prophets what He intended to do, and that's what He will do. The Lord God has already spoken and that is what He will do.

He is saving this country. He is bringing us in, and has brought us in, to a new era of peace and prosperity this world has never known as He makes room for His end-time harvest.

Again, "the Sovereign Lord does nothing without revealing His plan to His servants the prophets" (Amos 3:7). When God does something in the earth, He doesn't leave people in the dark; His prophets usually have a sense of under-standing about what will happen.

This vision reveals that God's greater plan is the end-time harvest. The prosperity and peace mentioned here are in preparation for a global outpouring in which multitudes will come to Christ.

God has and is continuing to work through this nation to be a blessing to the rest of the world. He has saved America for another season!

Part Four

2023 / Dawn

Section Notes

If you noticed during 2023, I only received one prophetic word. The Lord did not communicate any prophetic words for me to release to the "world." He did talk to me, but nothing like what I have been sharing.

I questioned why He got quiet. I sought Him for more words, and I even thought I was doing something wrong. I thought maybe He had stopped using me in the office of the prophet He answered me by saying, "Rehearse what I have already said."

He wanted me to go back and read through all the previous messages and go over them repeatedly. What more did He really have to share during that time? Those messages pretty well lay out the plan.

He also commanded me to "Part the waters and go to the other side" and to "Take as many people as I could." He wanted to send us ahead into the new era and begin working on that. He was leaving a few prophets back on the other side to encourage the stragglers with fresh words.

Looking back now, I can see His wisdom in this. There are times where God speaks loudly and frequently, and there are also times where He wants us to anchor ourselves in what has already been said.

It's amazing how, after all the previous years of walking by faith and showing up, I was still slow to grasp what He wanted me to do. Yet still, even in what seemed like silence, He was leading.

Chapter 23

My Power and Might Shall be Made Known

May 25, 2023

ALTHOUGH GOD HAD BEEN SPEAKING to me regularly, there was a period of time where I only received one prophetic word from Him. This prophetic word was a repeat message of an earlier word given on February 14, 2022. I've learned that when God repeats Himself, it's never an accident.

Repetition is God's way of emphasizing the importance of something. It's also an assurance that the thing He has spoken about will come to pass. The heart of this message emphasizes, once again, that God is confronting wickedness while raising up and renewing His faithful.

- *The Message* -

God is not playing around as it relates to evil and the wicked schemes concocted and implemented by evil men. The wrath of God is their lot now.

"They chose a path that was not My will. They wanted nothing to do with Me or righteousness. I have spoken, I have warned, I have held out My hand. They wanted to go on in their wickedness.

They make sport of their folly, even after they can see the warning signs of impending judgment and knowing full well their plans will ultimately fail and come to naught by My power. Yet they persist! They see the people arising, they see My hand unraveling their schemes, and they go on to their destruction."

In Psalms 2, we see the nations conspiring against God, but He laughs at them because He knows their schemes are futile. We are also warned in Proverbs 14:12 that there is a way that appears right to us, "but in the end it leads to death."

"I, the Lord, have spoken from My heavenly dwelling place. I have commanded and it shall be carried out. My plan shall stand," says the Lord of Hosts. "My ways shall be extended to all the earth."

"My power and might shall be known. Woe to the inhabitants of the earth who refuse my hand, My counsel, My mercy. Where will you hide? To whom will you run in the day of calamity? What can you offer Me to relent? I am the Almighty whom you turn your heels against.

For My faithful ones who continue to love and want My hand, YOU HAVE IT! I shall raise you up and no one shall bring you down anymore. Your name will be great in the earth as my representatives. Your heart shall be renewed and soar far above their calamity. Your life is in My hands and shall remain. I am yours and you are Mine. Ask what you will and see Me answer you! I love you. I am Your God! Continue in My ways and see Me all around you.

I, the Lord, have spoken!"

God repeating this word should indicate to us that we need to focus on it–not rush past it–and believe it. Many times, we want to hurry up and go to the next thing without fully absorbing and meditating on what we already have. Like kids who tear through the wrapping paper on Christmas morning, we can tend to look at God's words and toss them to the side, eager for the next word.

This is why I believe God gave this message again. The wicked will not succeed, no matter how long they appear to thrive. God's plan will prevail and His power and might will be experienced.

Part Five

2024 | The New Era

Section Notes

What an amazing God we worship and serve!

In this final section of this book. I hope you see the compilation of the previous messages and how it ties into the scriptures.

God is bringing this period to an end and bringing us into the next season and possibly the last season, we will see! However, only God knows the hour or the day of Jesus's return.

Be encouraged and see how God has stepped in to help us all!

Chapter 24

2020 Election: Never Seen Again

FEBRUARY 16, 2024

Many people don't believe God cares about politics, but that's simply not true. Some even think that pastors and ministry leaders should stay out of politics altogether. Yet politics involves policy, and policy affects people...people God cares about. Since God deeply cares for people, He would care about the things that shape their lives.

Our Lord and Savior is the King of Kings (both political titles). He has likewise called us kings and priests (Revelation 1:6), which also seem to be both political and religious titles. It is simply folly to believe that the One who gave Moses laws that governed the nation of Israel doesn't care about the governments that create laws in our world today. It would be worth re-reading this first part a second time.

However, the message in this prophetic word is clear: God will not ignore corruption and deception in these areas, nor in our personal affairs.

- The Message -

The Lord was never going to let that stand. It does not matter how many people were involved, nor how much money passed hands to hush people, help people look the other way, bribe people to take action to help, or be used to hire people to threaten. He was never going to just move on from it. This fraud and theft was to such a scale that it was never seen before and will never be seen again. There may be places that deal with cheating as is human fallen nature, but not to this scale.

God allowed them to do this so that He can expose them and it, and to show the people what has been going on underneath their noses for a long time. Godliness, purity, and righteousness does not just happen without efforts, thought, obedience and an active heart. If people don't work on it, they can revert or fall into a trap, into complacency, and into the fallen world. There is more to come on all of this. The Lord is not through. His ability to unravel even the best laid plans of men is wondrous. There is nothing hidden from the all-seeing, all-knowing, all-powerful, all-mighty God (Luke 8:17; Philippians 2:12; 1 Timothy 6:12).

Luke 8:17 tells us that there is nothing hidden that won't be known or brought into the open, and Philippians 2:12 tells us to work out our salvation with "fear and trembling." Lastly, 1 Timothy 6:12 tells us to fight the good fight of faith and actively resist the devil and corruption we encounter.

To do this, we must exercise vigilance. God is not done, and we will see how all this will unfold in the coming years. We can be confident that He will see this through to the end.

Chapter 25

The Time has Come

October 16, 2024

BY THE TIME this word came, I had not heard anything for a long time. This was because the previous year, God had already emphasized to me that I needed to meditate on what He had already spoken. For this reason, it didn't bother me as it had in the past. I spent hours, weeks and months receiving from the Lord what it has taken you just a few minutes to read! Take your time and let the message soak in.

This chapter takes place nearly four years after the second chapter of this book. Even just reading it and seeing what actually took place in real time is overwhelming (in a good way). I am very careful about prophetic words, and it's taken the Lord a long time to build up my confidence to publicly share words I feel like He's given me.

The timing of this word is so precious. Thank you, Lord, for trusting us with this message.

- The Message -

"The time has come to heal this land. Many are desperate for answers.

Many will be surprised at the results of the election, but not the righteous, who knew what God was going to do.

The transition will be determined by the prayers of God's people, the church, who indeed does have power to affect change on the earth. God's people, the righteous, must walk in faith and in their faithfulness. If you would like a certain result, are you willing to seek God for it, all the while doing your part?" (Luke 10:19; Habakkuk 2:4)

Luke 10:19 reminds believers of their authority, and Habakkuk 2:4 tells us the righteous will live by faith. This word calls the church to step into its God-given role to pray and expect God to move.

God works with His people. Do you know that it honors the Lord when we come to Him in faith, ask Him for His counsel, His advice, wait for it and take steps based on your faith in Him. Believing Him is one of the purest, best gifts you can give Him. If God says, 'ask,' and you don't, should you be disappointed in Him? Should you be frustrated with Him if He says, 'Seek and knock,' and you don't? (Matthew 7:7; Luke 11:9).

It is imperative, church, that we get this lesson. Other people's lives are counting on you, the church, to pray about everything. You have the power and permission to seek God for the answer, being peaceful if you have to wait. My people are destroyed for a lack of knowledge. People go astray without discernment (Philippians 4:6; Hosea 4:6).

"My bride! I do hear your pleas. I do see your dilemma. I have eyes to gaze upon your condition and situation. You may not fully know what I am doing from beginning to end, but it is for good! (Ecclesiastes 3:11)

Your time has come to push back against the darkness that has encroached on your land, your borders, and your morality. Your time to join together as one voice to speak and not be silent has come. Just because there is a new leader does not mean to sit idly by, basking in your win—but to advance the cause of

Christ to the nations. You have been brought through this time for such an agenda.

You don't all have to go to the same church. I gave a variety of families to be with. But you are part of a larger kingdom that is united as one. There is only one Lord, one faith, one baptism. Your personalities are different and wide-ranging, so I have a variety of individual families to be with all the while you come together as one family in Christ" (Ephesians 4:5-6).

God is stressing the importance of our partnership here. We are His "co-workers" in the work of the kingdom (1 Corinthians 3:9), and our job is to actively engage the culture around us. This section of the word is a mix of triumph and caution. The presidential win was not a finish line–it was a time of opportunity to take action. We may go to different churches and worship in different ways, but we still belong to one kingdom.

"My family, I do love you. I did this for you. Take the opportunity to teach your kids My truths. Take the opportunity to love the orphan, care for the sick, visit the prisoner, and serve your fellow man. Love without compromising the truth and righteous requirements of the gospel. Loving one another does not mean loving their failure or sin. Loving one another is, in fact, wanting them not to be lost forever. Care for people; use this season to do good. Plan for good. Bless one another. Seek good of one another—especially your fellow family member (the church). You have access to great resources—use them.

Ask for them—do NOT be ashamed to say "God, please help me." Do not be dismayed, to request God's presence and His counsel. You don't have because you don't ask.

Seek the Lord with all your heart no matter how prosperous you may become. It's not your wealth that makes you right with Me. It's not your treasure that keeps you safe—it's Me (Matthew 6:33).

Blessed are those who come to the truth and walk in the truth. Your days will be great upon the earth. Take the time to bless the Lord for all He has done. Go further in victory.

I, the Lord, have spoken."

Kevin Winkler

. . .

God is calling us to focus on seeking the kingdom of God and His righteousness (Matthew 6:33). This is a warning not to settle into a place of complacency. When we have the opportunity to get fat and lazy, we need to see it as a time of opportunity. This season being spoken of here is not a time to go relax, but to pull up our sleeves and do the things of God. The waiting is over and the time has come, but it will require prayer, unity, and action from the body of Christ. This is a time to advance the kingdom.

Chapter 26

Rest in the Lord

October 23, 2024

THIS PROPHETIC WORD was given before the physical events it described had unfolded. This is the true nature of prophecy; that God declares what He will do beforehand, and it is accomplished. Jeremiah 1:12 says, "I am watching to see that my word is fulfilled."

This message has hints of Israel's story: after God delivered them from Egypt, He commanded them to not just rejoice but to teach their children about Him and remember His works.

- The Message -

"O' My church. Rest in Me now. I have done what many thought impossible, but here you are. What does this mean? What is your response? Can I the Lord do what I say I will do? I fulfill My predetermined plan on the earth (Jeremiah 1:12).

Is My strength and power able to complete what I set out to do? You are witness to it. With your own eyes have you seen it.

Why am I doing these things for what purpose? Can you determine this?

Is it not for the future as well as for now. Who do your children say I AM? (Proverbs 22:6; Ephesians 6:4)

Do they even know the Lord? Do they comprehend My ways? Do they know Me?

Could this relief be also for them to hear about what God has done in your life-time? As I have done of old, I did now" (Psalms 78:4-7).

God is a God of the generations. He doesn't just want you to know Him; He wants your children and your children's children to know Him. In Ephesians 6:4, He commands fathers to bring up their children "in the training and instruction of the Lord." Likewise, Psalm 78:4-7 reminds parents to tell their children about God's deeds so they can trust in the Lord and keep His commands.

"I would have you teach your children My ways—to lean on, rely on and trust in Me, and to walk in faith and truth.

Your generation saw Me do the impossible to relent the enemy for a time.

Use this season to establish My ways upon the earth. As I have spoken, so I have done (Matthew 6:10).

Repent and return to your God, for He is good, kind, merciful and loving. He will hold you in the palm of His hand. But woe to him who does not return but plans to continue on in his ways. As a wild donkey cannot be broken, so are you (Acts 3:19; Psalms 145:8).

What can your Creator do but to let you go on in your ways to death. This was never My plan, or intention for you. But you don't want Me, so have it your way."

God does not want anyone to perish, yet some do. Psalm 145:8 reassures us that the Lord is "gracious and compassionate, slow to anger and rich in love." Unfortunately, those who stubbornly reject Him choose eternal separation, not because God wills it, but because they will not turn.

.   .   .

"For the rest, My lovely. Put forth your hands to be dressed in your wedding gown. How beautiful you are to Me. I long to provide for you, to care for you, to protect you—and to bring you safely to My side (Revelation 19:7-8).

Rest in Me as you go forth and conquer the land before you (Numbers 13:30).

I, the Lord, have spoken by My prophet."

The end of this word echoes Caleb's faith in Numbers 13:30, when he returned from scouting the enemies in the land and told Moses, "We should go up and take possession of the land, for we can certainly do it." God wants us to lean into Him. He has done what seemed impossible, and now it's our turn to rise and carry His kingdom forward.

God, you are so good to us. Thank you for saving us. Thank you for saving our little ones so that we might teach them. Help us, Father, to keep You first and spend all of our days living for You.

Chapter 27

Conquer the Land

December 26, 2024

THIS PROPHETIC WORD reminds us that God's heart toward His people has always been to love, bless, and care for us, and yet He also calls us to courage and obedience. He wants us to rise and conquer the land.

There are some instructions within this message that we should pause on. I think each one of us can receive them into our own lives and do them. Read and make note of what He might be asking you to do in this final season before the end.

- The Message -

"I want you to preach this.

I love the world I created. I love the creatures (man) I formed. It was My intention and heart to bless mankind all their days. They were to Me a source of immense pleasure (John 3:16).

I still care about the fate of the world and its inhabitants. It was never My desire to hurt them or allow them to be hurt. But man chooses his way. I want them to choose My way that I might take them up into My arms and care for them again (Psalms 25:4-12).

If a person wants Me (to love, fear and adore Him), they have nothing to fear (Isaiah 8:13).

It is I who hold all mercy in My hands (Romans 9:15-16).

It is I who can deliver you from all of your trials and troubles (Psalms 34:4).

It is I who can do it!

No one else is able to deliver you" (Isaiah 43:13).

The opening of this word is a reference to John 3:16, where we can see God's love for the world. He desires to bless us because He cares for us.

Isaiah 8:13 says, "The Lord Almighty is the one you are to regard as holy, He is the one you are to fear." Psalm 34:4 says, "I sought the Lord, and He answered me; He delivered me from all my fears." These verses serve to ground the church's confidence in God's mercy and His power.

"Go therefore and conquer the land. Who can stop you? (Numbers 13:30).

Who can win against you, if I have told you to do something? Who can thwart My plans that I have established and am establishing? What power is out there that can stop Me from being good to you, if I so choose?" (Romans 8:31; Deuteronomy 28:7; Jeremiah 1:19; Isaiah 41:12; Deuteronomy 20:4).

God expects His people to act with courage in the face of opposition. Romans 8:31 tells us that if God is for us, "who can be against us?" Deuteronomy 28:7 promises that enemies will come one way and flee seven ways, but Jeremiah 1:19 reminds us that opposition will not prevail. This is because God fights for His people (Deuteronomy 20:4).

"If you have a heart for Me, just ask and it will be yours. Share My love with others. I would like to bless them too. There is enough for all who want it. There is

no need to compare your life, calling, and ministry with anyone. Your life is your own and is unique to you and your experience; just as theirs is to them (Matthew 7:7; Galatians 6:4; 2 Corinthians 10:12).

Celebrate each other as unique. Help others see their value. Help others not compare. Help others keep their eyes on Jesus—He is always their source. He is their/your love (Hebrews 12:2).

Who can take your places in my plan?

I, the Lord, have spoken by my servant and friend—whom I love."

There is another theme that runs alongside the themes of righteousness, trust, and courage, and that is the theme of generosity. God desires to bless His people. He wants us to ask for what we need. He wants us to get what we need from a place of faith. In the Garden of Eden, there was no lack and God provided everything for Adam and Eve's enjoyment.

In heaven, there is also no lack because God provides everything for their enjoyment.

We must believe God's Word! If anything keeps us from believing that God wants to bless us and provide for us, we need to let go of it! We must start asking and believing Him! Let's get busy and conquer the land.

Regarding this particular prophetic word, God spoke a personal message to me because I believe it could also be for you. I felt that He said, "Share with them all of My messages and don't hold back. Life and liberty are within."

Jesus Is Lord!

Epilogue | The God Who Still Speaks

Thank you for joining me on this multi-year incredible journey of faith, trust, and hope. I really do hope that the Lord spoke to your heart during this trip together. I know that He is still speaking today and hope you have become keenly aware of that too.

As I reflect on the prophetic words the Lord released during these years, it is amazing to see it all from the "40,000-foot view." What are the threads of truth running through them?

- God loves His creation
- God cares about the affairs of men
- God is most certainly involved in our history
- He makes a distinction between those who love Him and those who do not
- He is merciful, but will judge
- He is gracious to forgive, but will punish unrepentant people
- He is not a respecter of people – rich or poor, political leaders or regular folks, famous or infamous – He is God over all
- He will do what He says He will do

We understand that not everything was fulfilled at the publishing of this book. But we have enough information to keep our eyes open and be watchful.

One of the biggest reasons God shares these supernatural messages ahead of time and then fulfills them before our eyes is for us to mature in faith.

What are things the Lord has shared in the Bible that have not come to pass yet? However, if God can bring President Trump back into the White House against all odds, and against what seemed to be a plan to prevent him from getting back in office by shooting him with a bullet in Butler, Pennsylvania– then what can He not do?

God is going to wrap up this age of the church like He said already, too.

There are two final outcomes for every person on earth: heaven with God (being saved) or hell without God (being lost). God desires to save everyone on earth. John 3:16 says:

For God so greatly loved and dearly prized the world that He [even] gave up His only begotten (unique) Son, so that whoever believes in (trusts in, clings to, relies on) Him shall not perish (come to destruction, be lost) but have eternal (everlasting) life. (AMPC)

Romans 10:10-17 says this:

For with the heart a person believes (adheres to, trusts in, and relies on Christ) and so is justified (declared righteous, acceptable to God), and with the mouth he confesses (declares openly and speaks out freely his faith) *and* confirms [his] salvation. The Scripture says, No man who believes in Him [who adheres to, relies on, and trusts in Him] will [ever] be put to shame *or* be disappointed. [No one] for there is no distinction between Jew and Greek. The same Lord is Lord over all [of us] and He generously bestows His riches upon all who call upon Him [in faith]. For everyone who calls upon the name of the Lord [invoking Him as Lord] will be saved. (AMPC)

Who is going to be your Lord? Someone will... Is it the devil? Yourself? Will it be the Lord Jesus Christ? If it's Him–declare that out of your mouth right now in Jesus' name!

If we believe a prophetic message about the exposure of corruption and that God wants to bless us if we ask, can we fully believe Him for our salvation by trusting in Jesus? This is the message of the gospel, or the good news, which is about Jesus's sacrifice on the cross for the world.

What about you? Have you already believed God about the good news? Have you called on the name of the Lord? Have you committed your life to Him? If you have, wonderful! Now let's help others do the same.

If you have not put your hope in Jesus, do you see a better time than right now? You do not have to be in a church or down at an altar somewhere to call on the name of the Lord–you can do it right now.

Do you believe what God said about His Son, Jesus? He was sent to this earth as a man to live a sinless life, was crucified on the cross, buried in a tomb and on the third day raised to life again. Do you believe Jesus is the Son of God? Do you believe in the man, Jesus Christ? Will you turn from your sins and repent of doing things your way? Will you ask the Lord to forgive you of your sins? Let Him help you live for Him from this minute forward!

Will you do that right now?

Don't delay, you may never get another chance!

Once a person breathes their last breath, there are no more chances and no more do-overs. It is wrong for some denominations to teach that there is salvation after death. Don't trust that; it's not biblical. Put your trust in God–right now!

If you made a decision to receive the gift of salvation, and from your heart asked Jesus to come into your heart and save you, tell someone about your new faith in Jesus. It's very important.

Tell a family member or friend or call us at 254-655-2171.

Write to us at pastor@thechurchalive.com–don't delay!

If you want to speak with a pastor about this or if you still need more information, call us, email us, or write us a letter. We are here for you. That's why we exist as a ministry.

If you still need help understanding why you should repent, or why God would sentence people to separation from Him (death/hell). We are as close as the internet, phone and post office. Contact us!

If you still need help. There is a very incredible organization who can share with you through video materials this so clearly. The organization is LivingWaters.org, and you can find them on YouTube.

He who has ears to hear, let him hear what the Spirit is saying.

The Lord is still speaking today. Listen, obey, and walk with Him.

Contact Information

I hope that you are encouraged by this book. I hope that you will keep showing up before the Lord all your days. We may never meet in-person. But if you want to contact me, I would love to hear from you. I would love to hear your story and testimony. If you want to write:

Church Alive
PO Box 253
China Spring, TX 76633
254-655-2171

Email me: pastor@thechurchalive.com

Other resources:

www.thechurchalive.com
www.AliveMediaNetwork.tv
www.WinklerWritingEnterprise.com

Watch shows and messages including a video message from each chapter of this book on **YouTube** @ ALIVE MEDIA NETWORK or Roku at Alive Media Network–the Prophetic Series

Contact Information

If you would like Kevin Winkler to speak to your group, email, call us, or write to us.

For more books by Kevin Winkler check out: Walls of Water

Available directly from us. Email us at pastor@thechurchalive.com or on Amazon.

www.ingramcontent.com/pod-product-compliance
Lightning Source LLC
Chambersburg PA
CBHW080902120626
46555CB00008B/2924